"WILD HORSES!"

Wordless and pale, the men examined their Sharps, and made ready to follow Jones. He slipped into the thorny brake and, flat on his stomach, wormed his way like a snake far into the thickly interlaced web of branches. Rude and Adams crawled after him. Words were superfluous.

Quiet, breathless, with beating hearts, the hunters pressed close to the dry grass. A long, low, steady rumble filled the air, and increased in volume till it became a roar.

Moments, endless moments, passed.

The roar filled out like a flood slowly released from its confines to sweep down with the sound of doom. The ground began to tremble and quake; the light faded; the smell of dust pervaded the thicket; then a continuous streaming roar, deafening as persistent roll of thunder, pervaded the hiding place.

"Lie low! lie low!" breathed the plainsman to his companions.

THE LAST OF THE PLAINSMEN

Zane Grey

BANTAM BOOKS
NEW YORK · TORONTO · LONDON · SYDNEY · AUCKLAND

*This edition contains the complete text
of the original hardcover edition.*
NOT ONE WORD HAS BEEN OMITTED.

THE LAST OF THE PLAINSMEN

A Bantam Book / July 1990

PRINTING HISTORY
Originally published in 1908

ISBN 0-553-28546-7

Published simultaneously in the United States and Canada

---

*Bantam Books are published by Bantam Books, a division of Bantam
Doubleday Dell Publishing Group, Inc. Its trademark, consisting of
the words "Bantam Books" and the portrayal of a rooster, is
Registered in U.S. Patent and Trademark Office and in other
countries. Marca Registrada. Bantam Books, 666 Fifth Avenue, New
York, New York 10103.*

PRINTED IN THE UNITED STATES OF AMERICA

RAD   0 9 8 7 6 5 4 3 2 1

Prefatory Note

As civilization encroached upon the plains Buffalo Jones ranged slowly westward; and to-day an isolated desert-bound plateau on the north rim of the Grand Cañon of Arizona is his home. There his buffalo browse with the mustang and deer, and are as free as ever they were on the rolling plains.

In the spring of 1907 I was the fortunate companion of the old plainsman on a trip across the desert, and a hunt in that wonderful country of yellow crags, deep cañons and giant pines. I want to tell about it. I want to show the color and beauty of those painted cliffs and the long, brown-matted bluebell-dotted aisles in the grand forests; I want to give a suggestion of the tang of the dry, cool air; and particularly I want to throw a little light upon the life and nature of that strange character and remarkable man, Buffalo Jones.

Happily in remembrance a writer can live over his experiences, and see once more the moon-blanched silver mountain peaks against the dark blue sky; hear the lonely sough of the nightwind through the pines; feel the dance of wild expectation in the quivering pulse; the stir, the thrill, the joy of hard action in perilous moments; the mystery of man's yearning for the unattainable.

As a boy I read of Boone with a throbbing heart, and the silent moccasined, vengeful Wetzel I loved. I pored over the deeds of later men—Custer and Carson, those heroes of the plains. And as a man I came to see the wonder, the tragedy of their lives, and to write about them. It has been my destiny—what a happy fulfillment of my dreams of border spirit!—to live for a while in the fast-fading wild environment which produced these great men with the last of the great plainsmen.

ZANE GREY

Contents

THE LAST
OF THE
PLAINSMEN

1

The Arizona Desert

One afternoon, far out on the sun-baked waste of sage, we made camp near a clump of withered piñon trees. The cold desert wind came down upon us with the sudden darkness. Even the Mormons, who were finding the trail for us across the drifting sands, forgot to sing and pray at sundown. We huddled round the campfire, a tired and silent little group. When out of the lonely, melancholy night some wandering Navajos stole like shadows to our fire, we hailed their advent with delight. They were good-natured Indians, willing to barter a blanket or bracelet; and one of them, a tall, gaunt fellow, with the bearing of a chief, could speak a little English.

"How," said he, in a deep chest voice.

"Hello, Noddlecoddy," greeted Jim Emmett, the Mormon guide.

"Ugh!" answered the Indian.

"Big paleface—Buffalo Jones—big chief—buffalo man," introduced Emmett, indicating Jones.

"How." The Navajo spoke with dignity, and extended a friendly hand.

"Jones big white chief—rope buffalo—tie up tight," continued Emmett, making motions with his arm, as if he were whirling a lasso.

"No big—heap small buffalo," said the Indian, holding his hand level with his knee, and smiling broadly.

Jones, erect, rugged, brawny, stood in the full light of

1

the campfire. He had a dark, bronzed, inscrutable face; a stern mouth and square jaw, keen eyes, half-closed from years of searching the wide plains, and deep furrows wrinkling his cheeks. A strange stillness enfolded his features—the tranquility earned from a long life of adventure.

He held up both muscular hands to the Navajo, and spread out his fingers.

"Rope buffalo—heap big buffalo—heap many—one sun."

The Indian straightened up, but kept his friendly smile.

"Me big chief," went on Jones, "me go far north—Land of Little Sticks—Naza! Naza!—rope musk-ox; rope White Manitou of Great Slaves—Naza! Naza!"

"Naza!" replied the Navajo, pointing to the North Star; "no—no."

"Yes—me big paleface—me come long way toward setting sun—go cross Big Water—go Buckskin—Siwash—chase cougar."

The cougar, or mountain lion, is a Navajo god and the Navajos hold him in as much fear and reverence as do the Great Slave Indians the musk-ox.

"No kill cougar," continued Jones, as the Indian's bold features hardened. "Run cougar horseback—run long way—dogs chase cougar long time—chase cougar up tree! Me big chief—me climb tree—climb high up—lasso cougar—rope cougar—tie cougar all tight."

The Navajo's solemn face relaxed.

"White man heap fun. No."

"Yes," cried Jones, extending his great arms. "Me strong; me rope cougar—me tie cougar; ride off wigwam, keep cougar alive."

"No," replied the savage vehemently.

"Yes," protested Jones, nodding earnestly.

"No," answered the Navajo, louder, raising his dark head.

"Yes!" shouted Jones.

"BIG LIE!" the Indian thundered.

Jones joined good-naturedly in the laugh at his expense. The Indian had crudely voiced a skepticism I had heard more delicately hinted in New York, and singularly enough, which had strengthened on our way West, as we met ranchers, prospectors and cowboys. But those few men I had fortunately met, who really knew Jones, more than overbalanced the doubt and ridicule cast upon him. I recalled a scarred old veteran of the plains, who had talked to me in true Western bluntness:

"Say, young feller, I heerd yer couldn't git acrost the cañon fer the deep snow on the north rim. Wal, ye're lucky. Now, yer hit the trail fer New York, an' keep goin'! Don't ever tackle the desert, 'specially with them Mormons. They've got water on the brain, wusser 'n religion. It's two hundred an' fifty miles from Flagstaff to Jones range, an' only two drinks on the trail. I know this hyar Buffalo Jones. I knowed him way back in the seventies, when he was doin' them ropin' stunts thet made him famous as the preserver of the American bison. I know about that crazy trip of his'n to the Barren Lands, after musk-ox. An' I reckon I kin guess what he'll do over there in the Siwash. He'll rope cougars—sure he will—an' watch 'em jump. Jones would rope the devil, an' tie him down if the lasso didn't burn. Oh! he's hell on ropin' things. An' he's wusser 'n hell on men, an' hosses, an' dogs."

All that my well-meaning friend suggested made me, of course, only the more eager to go with Jones. Where I had once been interested in the old buffalo hunter, I was now fascinated. And now I was with him in the desert and seeing him as he was, a simple, quiet man, who fitted the mountains and the silences and the long reaches of distance.

"It does seem hard to believe—all this about Jones," remarked Judd, one of Emmett's men. "How could a man have the strength and the nerve? And isn't it cruel to keep wild animals in captivity? Isn't it against God's word?"

Quick as speech could flow, Jones quoted: "And God said, 'Let us make man in our image, and give him dominion over the fish of the sea, the fowls of the air, over all the cattle, and over every creeping thing that creepeth upon the earth'!"

"Dominion—over all the beasts of the field!" repeated Jones, his big voice rolling out. He clenched his huge fists, and spread wide his long arms. "Dominion! That was God's word!" The power and intensity of him could be felt. Then he relaxed, dropped his arms, and once more grew calm. But he had shown a glimpse of the great, strange and absorbing passion of his life. Once he had told me how, when a mere child, he had hazarded limb and neck to capture a fox squirrel, how he had held on to the vicious little animal, though it bit his hand through; how he had never learned to play the games of boyhood; that when the youths of the little Illinois village were at play, he roamed the prairies, or the rolling, wooded hills, or watched a gopher hole. That boy was father of the man: for sixty years an enduring passion for dominion over wild animals had possessed him, and made his life an endless pursuit.

Our guests, the Navajos, departed early, and vanished silently in the gloom of the desert. We settled down again into a quiet that was broken only by the low chant-like song of a praying Mormon. Suddenly the hounds bristled, and old Moze, a surly and aggressive dog, rose and barked at some real or imaginary desert prowler. A sharp command from Jones made Moze crouch down, and the other hounds cowered close together.

"Better tie up the dogs," suggested Jones. "Like as not coyotes run down here from the hills."

The hounds were my especial delight. But Jones regarded them with considerable contempt. When all was said, this was no small wonder, for that quintet of long-eared canines would have tried the patience of a saint. Old Moze was a Missouri hound that Jones had procured in that State of uncertain qualities; and the dog had grown old over coontrails. He was black and white, grizzled and battle-scarred; and if ever a dog had an evil eye, Moze was that dog. He had a way of wagging his tail—an indeterminate, equivocal sort of wag, as if he realized his ugliness and knew he stood little chance of making friends, but was still hopeful and willing. As for me, the first time he manifested this evidence of a good heart under a rough coat, he won me forever.

To tell of Moze's derelictions up to that time would take more space than would a history of the whole trip; but the enumeration of several incidents will at once stamp him as a dog of character, and will establish the fact that even if his progenitors had never taken any blue ribbons, they had at least bequeathed him fighting blood. At Flagstaff we chained him in the yard of a livery stable. Next morning we found him hanging by his chain on the other side of an eight-foot fence. We took him down, expecting to have the sorrowful duty of burying him; but Moze shook himself, wagged his tail, and then pitched into the livery stable dog. As a matter of fact, fighting was his forte. He whipped all of the dogs in Flagstaff; and when our bloodhounds came on from California, he put three of them *hors de combat* at once, and subdued the pup with a savage growl. His crowning feat, however, made even the stoical Jones open his mouth in amaze. We had taken Moze to the El Tovar at the Grand Cañon, and finding it impossible to get over to the north rim, we left him with one of Jones's men, called Rust, who was working on the cañon trail. Rust's instructions were to bring Moze to Flagstaff in two weeks. He brought the dog a little ahead of time, and roared his appreciation of the relief it was to get the responsibility off his hands. And he related many strange things, most striking of which was how Moze had broken his chain and plunged into the raging Colorado River, and tried to swim it just above the terrible Sockdolager Rapids. Rust and his fellow-workmen watched the dog disappear in the yellow, wrestling, turbulent whirl of waters, and had heard his knell in the booming roar of the falls. Nothing but a fish could live in that current; nothing but a bird could scale those perpendicular marble walls. That night, however, when the men crossed on the tramway, Moze met them with a wag of his tail. He had crossed the river, and he had come back!

To the four reddish-brown, big-framed bloodhounds I had given the names of Don, Tige, Jude and Ranger; and by dint of persuasion, had succeeded in establishing some kind of family relation between them and Moze. This night I tied up the bloodhounds, after bathing and salving their sore feet; and I left Moze free, for he grew fretful and surly under restraint.

The Mormons, prone, dark, blanketed figures, lay on the sand. Jones was crawling into his bed. I walked a little way from the dying fire, and faced the north, where the desert stretched, mysterious and illimitable. How solemn and still it was! I drew in a great breath of the cold air, and thrilled with a nameless sensation. Something was there, away to the northward; it called to me from out of the dark and gloom; I was going to meet it.

I lay down to sleep with the great blue expanse open to my eyes. The stars were very large, and wonderfully bright, yet they seemed so much farther off than I had ever seen them. The wind softly sifted the sand. I hearkened to the tinkle of the cowbells on the hobbled horses. The last thing I remembered was old Moze creeping close to my side, seeking the warmth of my body.

When I awakened, a long, pale line showed out of the dun-colored clouds in the east. It slowly lengthened, and tinged to red. Then the morning broke, and the slopes of snow on the San Francisco peaks behind us glowed a delicate pink. The Mormons were up and doing with the dawn. They were stalwart men, rather silent, and all workers. It was interesting to see them pack for the day's journey. They traveled with wagons and mules, in the most primitive way, which Jones assured me was exactly as their fathers had crossed the plains fifty years before, on the trail to Utah.

All morning we made good time, and as we descended into the desert, the air became warmer, the scrubby cedar growth began to fail, and the bunches of sage were few and far between. I turned often to gaze back at the San Francisco peaks. The snowcapped tips glistened and grew higher, and stood out in startling relief. Some one said they could be seen two hundred miles across the desert, and were a landmark and a fascination to all travelers thitherward.

I never raised my eyes to the north that I did not draw my breath quickly and grow chill with awe and bewilderment with the marvel of the desert. The scaly red ground descended gradually; bare red knolls, like waves, rolled away northward; black buttes reared their flat heads; long ranges of sand flowed between them like streams, and all sloped away to merge into gray, shadowy obscurity, into wild and desolate, dreamy and misty nothingness.

"Do you see those white sand dunes there, more to the left?" asked Emmett. "The Little Colorado runs in there. How far does it look to you?"

"Thirty miles, perhaps," I replied, adding ten miles to my estimate.

"It's seventy-five. We'll get there day after to-morrow. If the snow in the mountains has begun to melt, we'll have a time getting across."

That afternoon, a hot wind blew in my face, carrying fine sand that cut and blinded. It filled my throat, sending me to the water cask till I was ashamed. When I fell into my bed at night, I never turned. The next day was hotter; the wind blew harder; the sand stung sharper.

About noon the following day, the horses whinnied, and the mules roused out of their tardy gait. "They smell water," said Emmett. And despite the heat, and the sand in my nostrils, I smelled it, too. The dogs, poor foot-sore fellows, trotted on ahead down the trail. A few more miles of hot sand and gravel and red stone brought us around a low mesa to the Little Colorado.

It was a wide stream of swiftly running, reddish-muddy water. In the channel, cut by floods, little streams trickled and meandered in all directions. The main part of the river ran in close to the bank we were on. The dogs lolled in the water; the horses and mules tried to run in, but were restrained; the men drank, and bathed their faces. According to my Flagstaff adviser, this was one of the two drinks I would get on the desert, so I availed myself heartily of the opportunity. The water was full of sand, but cold and gratefully thirst-quenching.

The Little Colorado seemed no more to me than a shallow creek; I heard nothing sullen or menacing in its musical flow.

"Doesn't look bad, eh?" queried Emmett, who read my thought. "You'd be surprised to learn how many men and

Indians, horses, sheep and wagons are buried under that quicksand."

The secret was out, and I wondered no more. At once the stream and wet bars of sand took on a different color. I removed my boots, and waded out to a little bar. The sand seemed quite firm, but water oozed out around my feet; and when I stepped, the whole bar shook like jelly. I pushed my foot through the crust, and the cold, wet sand took hold, and tried to suck me down.

"How can you ford this stream with horses?" I asked Emmett.

"We must take our chances," replied he. "We'll hitch two teams to one wagon, and run the horses. I've forded here at worse stages than this. Once a team got stuck, and I had to leave it; another time the water was high, and washed me downstream."

Emmett sent his son into the stream on a mule. The rider lashed his mount, and plunging, splashing, crossed at a pace near a gallop. He returned in the same manner, and reported one bad place near the other side.

Jones and I got on the first wagon and tried to coax up the dogs, but they would not come. Emmett had to lash the four horses to start them; and other Mormons riding alongside, yelled at them, and used their whips. The wagon bowled into the water with a tremendous splash. We were wet through before we had gone twenty feet. The plunging horses were lost in yellow spray; the stream rushed through the wheels; the Mormons yelled. I wanted to see, but was lost in a veil of yellow mist. Jones yelled in my ear, but I could not hear what he said. Once the wagon wheels struck a stone or log, almost lurching us overboard. A muddy splash blinded me. I cried out in my excitement, and punched Jones in the back. Next moment, the keen exhilaration of the ride gave way to horror. We seemed to drag, and almost stop. Some one roared: "Horse down!" One instant of painful suspense, in which imagination pictured another tragedy added to the record of this deceitful river—a moment filled with intense feeling, and sensation of splash, and yell, and fury of action: then the three able horses dragged their comrade out of the quicksand. He regained his feet, and plunged on. Spurred by fear, the horses increased their efforts, and amid clouds of spray, galloped the remaining distance to the other side.

Jones looked disgusted. Like all plainsmen, he hated water. Emmett and his men calmly unhitched. No trace of alarm, or even of excitement showed in their bronzed faces.

"We made that fine and easy," remarked Emmett.

So I sat down and wondered what Jones and Emmett, and these men would consider really hazardous. I began to have a feeling that I would find out; that experience for me was but in its infancy; that far across the desert the something which had called me would show hard, keen, perilous life. And I began to think of reserve powers of fortitude and endurance.

The other wagons were brought across without mishap; but the dogs did not come with them. Jones called and called. The dogs howled and howled. Finally I waded out over the wet bars and little streams to a point several hundred yards nearer the dogs. Moze was lying down, but the others were whining and howling in a state of great perturbation. I called and called. They answered, and even ran into the water, but did not start across.

"Hyah, Moze! hyah, you Indian!" I yelled, losing my patience. "You've already swum the Big Colorado, and this is only a brook. Come on!"

This appeal evidently touched Moze, for he barked, and plunged in. He made the water fly, and when carried off his feet, breasted the current with energy and power. He made shore almost even with me, and wagged his tail. Not to be out-done, Jude, Tige and Don followed suit, and first one and then another was swept off his feet and carried downstream. They landed below me. This left Ranger, the pup, alone on the other shore. Of all the pitiful yelps ever uttered by a frightened and lonely puppy, his were the most forlorn I had ever heard. Time after time he plunged in, and with many bitter howls of distress, went back. I kept calling, and at last, hoping to make him come by a show of indifference, I started away. This broke his heart. Putting up his head, he let out a long, melancholy wail, which for aught I knew might have been a prayer, and then consigned himself to the yellow current. Ranger swam like a boy learning. He seemed to be afraid to get wet. His forefeet were continually pawing the air in front of his nose. When he struck the swift place, he went downstream, like a flash, but still kept swimming valiantly. I tried to follow along the sand-bar, but found it impossible. I encouraged him by yelling. He drifted far below, stranded on an island, crossed it, and plunged in again, to make shore almost out of my sight. And when at last I got to dry sand, there was Ranger, wet and disheveled, but consciously proud and happy.

After lunch we entered upon the seventy-mile stretch from the Little to the Big Colorado.

Imagination had pictured the desert for me as a vast, sandy plain, flat and monotonous. Reality showed me desolate mountains gleaming bare in the sun, long lines of red bluffs, white sand dunes, and hills of blue clay, areas of level ground—in all, a many-hued, boundless world in itself, wonderful and beautiful, fading all around into the purple haze of deceiving distance.

Thin, clear, sweet, dry, the desert air carried a languor, a dreaminess, tidings of far-off things, and an enthralling promise. The fragrance of flowers, the beauty and grace of women, the sweetness of music, the mystery of life—all seemed to float on that promise. It was the air breathed by the lotus-eaters, when they dreamed, and wandered no more.

Beyond the Little Colorado, we began to climb again. The sand was thick; the horses labored; the drivers shielded their faces. The dogs began to limp and lag. Ranger had to be taken into a wagon; and then, one by one, all of the other dogs except Moze. He refused to ride, and trotted along with his head down.

Far to the front the pink cliffs, the ragged mesas, the dark, volcanic spurs of the Big Colorado stood up and beckoned us onward. But they were a far hundred miles across the shifting sands, and baked clay, and ragged rocks. Always in the rear rose the San Francisco peaks, cold and pure, startlingly clear and close in the rare atmosphere.

We camped near another water hole, located in a deep, yellow-colored gorge, crumbling to pieces, a ruin of rock, and silent as the grave. In the bottom of the cañon was a pool of water, covered with green scum. My thirst was effectually quenched by the mere sight of it. I slept poorly, and lay for hours watching the great stars. The silence was painfully oppressive. If Jones had not begun to give a respectable imitation of the exhaust pipe on a steamboat, I should have been compelled to shout aloud, or get up; but this snoring would have dispelled anything. The morning came gray and cheerless. I got up stiff and sore, with a tongue like a rope.

All day long we ran the gauntlet of the hot, flying sand. Night came again, a cold, windy night. I slept well until a mule stepped on my bed, which was conducive to restlessness. At dawn, cold, gray clouds tried to blot out the rosy east. I could hardly get up. My lips were cracked; my tongue swollen to twice its natural size; my eyes smarted and burned. The barrels and kegs of water were exhausted. Holes that had been dug in the dry sand of a dry stream-bed the night before in the morning yielded a scant supply of muddy alkali water, which went to the horses.

Only twice that day did I rouse to anything resembling enthusiasm. We came to a stretch of country showing the wonderful diversity of the desert land. A long range of beautiful rounded clay dunes bordered the trail. So symmetrical were they that I imagined them works of sculptors. Light blue, dark blue, clay blue, marine blue, cobalt blue—every shade of blue was there, but no other color. The other time that I awoke to sensations from without was when we came to the top of a ridge. We had been passing through red-lands. Jones called the place a strong, specific word which really was illustrative of the heat amid those scaling red ridges. We came out where the red changed abruptly to gray. I seemed always to see things first, and I cried out: "Look! here are a red lake and trees!"

"No, lad, not a lake," said old Jim, smiling at me; "that's what haunts the desert traveler. It's only a mirage!"

So I awoke to the realization of that illusive thing, the mirage, a beautiful lie, false as stairs of sand. Far northward a clear rippling lake sparkled in the sunshine. Tall, stately trees, with waving green foliage, bordered the water. For a long moment it lay there, smiling in the sun, a thing almost tangible; and then it faded. I felt a sense of actual loss. So real had been the illusion that I could not believe I was not soon to drink and wade and dabble in the cool waters. Disappointment was keen. This is what maddens the prospector or sheep-herder lost in the desert. Was it not a terrible thing to be dying of thirst, to see sparkling water, almost to smell it, and then realize suddenly that all was only a lying trick of the desert, a lure, a delusion? I ceased to wonder at the Mormons, and their search for water, their talk of water. But I had not realized its true significance. I had not known what water was. I had never appreciated it. So it was my destiny to learn that water is the greatest thing on earth. I hung over a three-foot hole in a dry stream-bed, and watched it ooze and seep through the sand, and fill up—oh, so slowly; and I felt it loosen my parched tongue, and steal through all my dry body with strength and life. Water is said to constitute three fourths of the universe. However that may be, on the desert it is the whole world, and all of life.

Two days passed by, all hot sand and wind and glare. The Mormons sang no more at evening; Jones was silent; the dogs were limp as rags.

At Moncáupie Wash we ran into a sandstorm. The horses turned their backs to it, and bowed their heads patiently. The Mormons covered themselves. I wrapped a blanket round my head and hid behind a sage bush. The wind, carrying the sand, made a strange hollow roar. All was enveloped in a weird yellow opacity. The sand seeped through the sage bush and swept by with a soft, rustling sound, not unlike the wind in the rye. From time to time I raised a corner of my blanket and peeped out. Where my feet had stretched was an enormous mound of sand. I felt the blanket, weighted down, slowly settle over me.

Suddenly as it had come, the sandstorm passed. It left a changed world for us. The trail was covered; the wheels hub-deep in sand; the horses, walking sand dunes. I could not close my teeth without grating harshly on sand.

We journeyed onward, and passed long lines of petrified trees, some a hundred feet in length, lying as they had fallen, thousands of years before. White ants crawled among the ruins. Slowly climbing the sandy trail, we circled a great red bluff with jagged peaks, that had seemed an interminable obstacle. A scant growth of cedar and sage again made its appearance. Here we halted to pass another night. Under a cedar I heard the plaintive, piteous bleat of an animal. I searched, and presently found a little black and white lamb, scarcely able to stand. It came readily to me, and I carried it to the wagon.

"That's a Navajo lamb," said Emmett. "It's lost. There are Navajo Indians close by."

"'Away in the desert we heard its cry,'" quoted one of the Mormons.

Jones and I climbed the red mesa near camp to see the sunset. All the western world was ablaze in golden glory. Shafts of light shot toward the zenith, and bands of paler gold, tinging to rose, circled away from the fiery, sinking globe. Suddenly the sun sank, the gold changed to gray, then to purple, and shadows formed in the deep gorge at our feet. So sudden was the transformation that soon it was night, the solemn, impressive night of the desert. A stillness that seemed too sacred to break clasped the place; it was infinite; it held the bygone ages, and eternity.

More days, and miles, miles, miles! The last day's ride to the Big Colorado was unforgettable. We rode toward the head of a gigantic red cliff pocket, a veritable inferno, immeasurably hot, glaring, awful. It towered higher and higher above us. When we reached a point of this red barrier, we heard the dull rumbling roar of water, and we came out, at length, on a winding trail cut in the face of a bluff overhanging the Colorado River. The first sight of most famous and much-heralded wonders of nature is often disappointing; but never can this be said of the blood-hued Rio Colorado. If it had beauty, it was beauty that appalled. So riveted was my gaze that I could hardly turn it across the river, where Emmett proudly pointed out his lonely home—an oasis set down amidst beetling red cliffs. How grateful to the eye was the green of alfalfa and cottonwood! Going round the bluff trail, the wheels had only a foot of room to spare; and the sheer descent into the red, turbid, congested river was terrifying.

I saw the constricted rapids, where the Colorado took its plunge into the box-like head of the Grand Cañon of Arizona; and the deep, reverberating boom of the river, at flood height, was a fearful thing to hear. I could not repress a shudder at the thought of crossing above that rapid.

The bronze walls widened as we proceeded, and we got down presently to a level, where a long wire cable stretched across the river. Under the cable ran a rope. On the other side was an old scow moored to the bank.

"Are we going across in that?" I asked Emmett, pointing to the boat.

"We'll all be on the other side before dark," he replied cheerily.

I felt that I would rather start back alone over the desert than trust myself in such a craft, on such a river. And it was all because I had had experience with bad rivers, and thought I was a judge of dangerous currents. The Colorado slid with a menacing roar out of a giant split in the red wall, and whirled, eddied, bulged on toward its confinement in the iron-ribbed cañon below.

In answer to shots fired, Emmett's man appeared on the other side, and rode down to the ferry landing. Here he got into a skiff, and rowed laboriously upstream for a long distance before he started across, and then swung into the current. He swept down rapidly, and twice the skiff whirled, and completely turned round; but he reached our bank safely. Taking two men aboard he rowed upstream again, close to the shore, and returned to the opposite side in much the same manner in which he had come over.

The three men pushed out the scow, and grasping the rope overhead, began to pull. The big craft ran easily. When the current struck it, the wire cable sagged, the water boiled and surged under it, raising one end, and then the other. Nevertheless, five minutes were all that were required to pull the boat over.

It was a rude, oblong affair, made of heavy planks loosely put together, and it leaked. When Jones suggested that we get the agony over as quickly as possible, I was with him, and we embarked together. Jones said he did not like the looks of the tackle; and when I thought of his by no means small mechanical skill, I had not added a cheerful idea to my consciousness. The horses of the first team had to be dragged upon the scow, and once on, they reared and plunged.

When we started, four men pulled the rope, and Emmett sat in the stern, with the tackle guys in hand. As the current hit us, he let out the guys, which maneuver caused the boat to swing stern down stream. When it pointed obliquely, he made fast the guys again. I saw that this served two purposes: the current struck, slid alongside, and over the stern, which mitigated the danger, and at the same time helped the boat across.

To look at the river was to court terror, but I had to look. It was an infernal thing. It roared in hollow, sullen voice, as a monster growling. It had a voice, this river, and one strangely changeful. It moaned as if in pain—it whined, it cried. Then at times it would seem strangely silent. The current was so complex and mutable as human life. It boiled, beat and bulged. The bulge itself was an incomprehensible thing, like a roaring lift of the waters from a submarine explosion. Then it would smooth out, and run like oil. It shifted from one channel to another, rushed to the center of the river, then swung close to one shore or the other. Again it swelled near the boat, in great, boiling, hissing eddies.

"Look! See where it breaks through the mountain!" yelled Jones in my ear.

I looked upstream to see the stupendous granite walls separated in a gigantic split that must have been made by a terrible seismic disturbance; and from this gap poured the dark, turgid, mystic flood.

I was in a cold sweat when we touched shore, and I jumped long before the boat was properly moored.

Emmett was wet to the waist where the water had surged over him. As he sat rearranging some tackle I remarked to him that of course he must be a splendid swimmer, or he would not take such risks.

"No, I can't swim a stroke," he replied; "and it wouldn't be any use if I could. Once in there a man's a goner."

"You've had bad accidents here?" I questioned.

"No, not bad. We only drowned two men last year. You see, we had to tow the boat up the river, and row across, as then we hadn't the wire. Just above, on this side, the boat hit a stone, and the current washed over her, taking off the team and two men."

"Didn't you attempt to rescue them?" I asked, after waiting a moment.

"No use. They never came up."

"Isn't the river high now?" I continued, shuddering as I glanced out at the whirling logs and drifts.

"High, and coming up. If I don't get the other teams over to-day I'll wait until she goes down. At this season she rises and lowers every day or so, until June; then comes the big flood, and we don't cross for months."

I sat for three hours watching Emmett bring over the rest of his party, which he did without accident, but at the expense of great effort. And all the time in my ears dinned the roar, the boom, the rumble of this singularly rapacious and purposeful river—a river of silt, a red river of dark, sinister meaning, a river with terrible work to perform, a river which never gave up its dead.

2

The Range

After a much-needed rest at Emmett's, we bade good-bye to him and his hospitable family, and under the guidance of his man once more took to the wind-swept trail. We pursued a southwesterly course now, following the lead of the craggy red wall that stretched on and on for hundreds of miles into Utah. The desert, smoky and hot, fell away to the left, and in the foreground a dark, irregular line marked the Grand Cañon cutting through the plateau.

The wind whipped in from the vast, open expanse, and meeting an obstacle in the red wall, turned north and raced past us. Jones's hat blew off, stood on its rim, and rolled. It kept on rolling, thirty miles an hour, more or less; so fast, at least, that we were a long time catching up to it with a team of horses. Possibly we never would have caught it had not a stone checked its flight. Further manifestation of the power of the desert wind surrounded us on all sides. It had hollowed out huge stones from the cliffs, and tumbled them to the plain below; and then, sweeping sand and gravel low across the desert floor, had cut them deeply, until they rested on slender pedestals, thus sculptoring grotesque and striking monuments to the marvelous persistence of this element of nature.

Late that afternoon, as we reached the height of the plateau, Jones woke up and shouted: "Ha! there's Buck-skin!"

Far southward lay a long, black mountain, covered with patches of shining snow. I could follow the zigzag line of the Grand Cañon splitting the desert plateau, and saw it disappear in the haze round the end of the mountain. From this I got my first clear impression of the topography of the country surrounding our objective point. Buckskin mountain ran its blunt end eastward to the cañon—in fact, formed a hundred miles of the north rim. As it was nine thousand feet high it still held the snow, which had occasioned our lengthy desert ride to get back of the mountain. I could see the long slopes rising out of the desert to meet the timber.

As we bowled merrily down grade I noticed that we were no longer on stony ground, and that a little scant silvery grass had made its appearance. Then little branches of green, with a blue flower, smiled out of the clayish sand.

All of a sudden Jones stood up, and let out a wild Comanche yell. I was more startled by the yell than by the great hand he smashed down on my shoulder, and for the moment I was dazed.

"There! look! look! the buffalo! Hi! Hi! Hi!"

Below us, a few miles on a rising knoll, a big herd of buffalo shone black in the gold of the evening sun. I had not Jones's incentive, but I felt enthusiasm born of the wild and beautiful picture, and added my yell to his. The huge, burly leader of the herd lifted his head, and after regarding us for a few moments calmly went on browsing.

The desert had fringed away into a grand rolling pastureland, walled in by the red cliffs, the slopes of Buckskin, and further isolated by the cañon. Here was a range of twenty-four hundred square miles without a foot of barb-wire, a pasture fenced in by natural forces, with the splendid feature that the buffalo could browse on the plain in winter, and go up into the cool foothills of Buckskin in summer.

From another ridge we saw a cabin dotting the rolling plain, and in half an hour we reached it. As we climbed down from the wagon a brown and black dog came dashing out of the cabin, and promptly jumped at Moze. His selection showed poor discrimination, for Moze whipped

him before I could separate them. Hearing Jones heartily
greeting some one, I turned in his direction, only to be
distracted by another dog fight. Don had tackled Moze for
the seventh time. Memory rankled in Don, and he needed
a lot of whipping, some of which he was getting when I
rescued him.

Next moment I was shaking hands with Frank and Jim,
Jones's ranchmen. At a glance I liked them both. Frank was
short and wiry, and had a big, ferocious mustache, the effect
of which was softened by his kindly brown eyes. Jim was
tall, a little heavier; he had a careless, tidy look; his eyes
were searching, and though he appeared a young man, his
hair was white.

"I shore am glad to see you all," said Jim, in slow, soft,
Southern accent.

"Get down, get down," was Frank's welcome—a typi-
cally Western one, for we had already gotten down; "an'
come in. You must be worked out. Sure you've come a long
way." He was quick of speech, full of nervous energy, and
beamed with hospitality.

The cabin was the rudest kind of log affair, with a huge
stone fireplace in one end, deer antlers and coyote skins on
the wall, saddles and cowboys' traps in a corner, a nice,
large, promising cupboard, and a table and chairs. Jim
threw wood on a smoldering fire, that soon blazed and
crackled cheerily.

I sank down into a chair with a feeling of blessed relief.
Ten days of desert ride behind me! Promise of wonderful
days before me, with the last of the old plainsmen! No
wonder a sweet sense of ease stole over me, or that the fire
seemed a live and joyously welcoming thing, or that Jim's
deft maneuvers in preparation of supper roused in me a
rapt admiration.

"Twenty calves this spring!" cried Jones, punching me
in my sore side. "Ten thousand dollars worth of calves!"

He was now altogether a changed man; he looked
almost young; his eyes danced, and he rubbed his big hands
together while he plied Frank with questions. In strange
surroundings—that is, away from his native wilds, Jones
had been a silent man; it had been almost impossible to get

anything out of him. But now I saw that I should come to know the real man. In a very few moments he had talked more than on all the desert trip, and what he said, added to the little I had already learned, put me in possession of some interesting information as to his buffalo.

Some years before he had conceived the idea of hybridizing buffalo with black Galloway cattle; and with the characteristic determination and energy of the man, he at once set about finding a suitable range. This was difficult, and took years of searching. At last the wild north rim of the Grand Cañon, a section unknown except to a few Indians and mustang hunters, was settled upon. Then the gigantic task of transporting the herd of buffalo by rail from Montana to Salt Lake was begun. The two hundred and ninety miles of desert lying between the home of the Mormons and Buckskins Mountain was an obstacle almost insurmountable. The journey was undertaken and found even more trying than had been expected. Buffalo after buffalo died on the way. Then Frank, Jones's right-hand man, put into execution a plan he had been thinking of—namely, to travel by night. It succeeded. The buffalo rested in the day and traveled by easy stages by night, with the result that the big herd was transported to the ideal range.

Here, in an environment strange to their race, but peculiarly adaptable, they thrived and multiplied. The hybrid of the Galloway cow and buffalo proved a great success. Jones called the new species "Cattalo." The cattalo took the hardiness of the buffalo, and never required artificial food or shelter. He would face the desert storm or blizzard and stand stock still in his tracks until the weather cleared. He became quite domestic, could be easily handled, and grew exceedingly fat on very little provender. The folds of his stomach were so numerous that they digested even the hardest and flintiest of corn. He had fourteen ribs on each side, while domestic cattle had only thirteen; thus he could endure rougher work and longer journeys to water. His fur was so dense and glossy that it equaled that of the unplucked beaver or otter, and was fully as valuable as the buffalo robe. And not to be overlooked by any means was the fact that his meat was delicious.

Jones had to hear every detail of all that had happened since his absence in the East, and he was particularly inquisitive to learn all about the twenty cattalo calves. He called different buffalo by name; and designated the calves by descriptive terms, such as "Whiteface" and "Crosspatch." He almost forgot to eat, and kept Frank too busy to get anything into his own mouth. After supper he calmed down.

"How about your other man—Mr. Wallace, I think you said?" asked Frank.

"We expected to meet him at Grand Cañon Station, and then at Flagstaff. But he didn't show up. Either he backed out or missed us. I'm sorry; for when we get up on Buckskin, among the wild horses and cougars, we'll be likely to need him."

"I reckon you'll need me, as well as Jim," said Frank dryly, with a twinkle in his eye. "The buffs are in good shape an' can get along without me for a while."

"That'll be fine. How about cougar sign on the mountain?"

"Plenty. I've got two spotted near Oak Spring. Comin' over two weeks ago I tracked them in the snow along the trail for miles. We'll ooze over that way, as it's goin' toward the Siwash. The Siwash breaks of the cañon—there's the place for lions. I met a wild-horse wrangler not long back, an' he was tellin' me about Old Tom an' the colts he'd killed this winter."

Naturally, I here expressed a desire to know more of Old Tom.

"He's the biggest cougar ever known of in these parts. His tracks are bigger than a horse's an' have been seen on Buckskin for twelve years. This wrangler—his name is Clark—said he'd turned his saddle horse out to graze near camp, an' Old Tom sneaked in an' downed him. The lions over there are sure a bold bunch. Well, why shouldn't they be? No one ever hunted them. You see, the mountain is hard to get at. But now you're here, if it's big cats you want we sure can find them. Only be easy, be easy. You've all the time there is. An' any job on Buckskin will take time. We'll look the calves over, an' you must ride the range to harden up. Then we'll ooze over toward Oak. I expect it'll be boggy, an' I hope the snow melts soon."

"The snow hadn't melted on Greenland point," replied Jones. "We saw that with a glass from the El Tovar. We wanted to cross that way, but Rust said Bright Angel Creek was breast high to a horse, and that creek is the trail."

"There's four feet of snow on Greenland," said Frank. "It was too early to come that way. There's only about three months in the year the cañon can be crossed at Greenland."

"I want to get in the snow," returned Jones. "This bunch of long-eared canines I brought never smelled a lion track. Hounds can't be trained quick without snow. You've got to see what they're trailing, or you can't break them."

Frank looked dubious. "'Pears to me we'll have trouble gettin' a lion without lion dogs. It takes a long time to break a hound off of deer, once he's chased them. Buckskin is full of deer, wolves, coyotes, and there's wild horses. We couldn't go a hundred feet without crossin' trails."

"How's the hound you and Jim fetched in last year? Has he got a good nose? Here he is—I like his head. Come here, Bowser—what's his name?"

"Jim named him Sounder, because he sure has a voice. It's great to hear him on a trail. Sounder has a nose that can't be fooled, an' he'll trail anythin'; but I don't know if he ever got up a lion."

Sounder wagged his bushy tail and looked up affectionately at Frank. He had a fine head, great brown eyes, very long ears and curly brownish-black hair. He was not demonstrative, looked rather askance at Jones, and avoided the other dogs.

"That dog will make a great lion-chaser," said Jones, decisively, after his study of Sounder. "He and Moze will keep us busy, once they learn we want lions."

"I don't believe any dog-trainer could teach them short of six months," replied Frank. "Sounder is no spring chicken; an' that black and dirty white cross between a cayuse an' a barb-wire fence is an old dog. You can't teach old dogs new tricks."

Jones smiled mysteriously, a smile of conscious superiority, but said nothing.

"We'll shore hev a storm to-morrow," said Jim, relinquishing his pipe long enough to speak. He had been silent, and now his meditative gaze was on the west, through the cabin window, where a dull afterglow faded under the heavy laden clouds of night and left the horizon dark.

I was very tired when I lay down, but so full of excitement that sleep did not soon visit my eyelids. The talk about buffalo, wild-horse hunters, lions and dogs, the prospect of hard riding and unusual adventure; the vision of Old Tom that had already begun to haunt me, filled my mind with pictures and fancies. The other fellows dropped off to sleep, and quiet reigned. Suddenly a succession of queer, sharp barks came from the plain, close to the cabin. Coyotes were paying us a call, and judging from the chorus of yelps and howls from our dogs, it was not a welcome visit. Above the medley rose one big, deep, full voice that I knew at once belonged to Sounder. Then all was quiet again. Sleep gradually benumbed my senses. Vague phrases dreamily drifted to and fro in my mind: "Jones's wild range—Old Tom—Sounder—great name—great voice—Sounder! Sounder! Sound——"

Next morning I could hardly crawl out of my sleeping-bag. My bones ached, my muscles protested excruciatingly, my lips burned and bled, and the cold I had contracted on the desert clung to me. A good brisk walk round the corrals, and then breakfast, made me feel better.

"Of course you can ride?" queried Frank.

My answer was not given from an overwhelming desire to be truthful. Frank frowned a little, as it wondering how a man could have the nerve to start out on a jaunt with Buffalo Jones without being a good horseman. To be unable to stick on the back of a wild mustang, or a cayuse, was an unpardonable sin in Arizona. My frank admission was made relatively, with my mind on what cowboys held as a standard of horsemanship.

The mount Frank trotted out of the corral for me was a pure white, beautiful mustang, nervous, sensitive, quivering. I watched Frank put on the saddle, and when he called me I did not fail to catch a covert twinkle in his merry brown eyes. Looking away toward Buckskin Mountain, which was coincidentally in the direction of home, I said to myself: "This may be where you get on, but most certainly it is where you get off!"

Jones was already riding far beyond the corral, as I could see by a cloud of dust; and I set off after him, with the painful consciousness that I must have looked to Frank and Jim much as Central Park equestrians had often looked to me. Frank shouted after me that he would catch up with us out on the range. I was not in any great hurry to overtake Jones, but evidently my horse's inclinations differed from mine; at any rate, he made the dust fly, and jumped the little sage bushes.

Jones, who had tarried to inspect one of the pools—formed of running water from the corrals—greeted me as I came up with this cheerful observation:

"What in thunder did Frank give you that white nag for? The buffalo hate white horses—anything white. They're liable to stampede off the range, or chase you into the cañon."

I replied grimly that, as it was certain something was going to happen, the particular circumstance might as well come off quickly.

We rode over the rolling plain with a cool, bracing breeze in our faces. The sky was dull and mottled with a beautiful cloud effect that presaged wind. As we trotted along Jones pointed out to me and descanted upon the nutritive value of three different kinds of grass, one of which he called the Buffalo Pea, noteworthy for a beautiful blue blossom. Soon we passed out of sight of the cabin, and could see only the billowy plain, the red tips of the stony wall, and the black-fringed crest of Buckskin. After riding a while we made out some cattle, a few of which were on the range, browsing in the lee of a ridge. No sooner had I marked them than Jones let out another Comanche yell.

"Wolf!" he yelled; and spurring his big bag, he was off like the wind.

A single glance showed me several cows running as if bewildered, and near them a big white wolf pulling down a calf. Another white wolf stood not far off. My horse jumped as if he had been shot; and the realization darted upon me

that here was where the certain something began. Spot—
the mustang had one black spot in his pure white—snorted
like I imagined a blooded horse might, under dire insult.
Jones's bay had gotten about a hundred paces the start. I
lived to learn that Spot hated to be left behind; moreover,
he would not be left behind; he was the swiftest horse on
the range, and proud of the distinction. I cast one unmen-
tionable word on the breeze toward the cabin and Frank,
then put mind and muscle to the sore task of remaining
with Spot. Jones was born on a saddle, and had been taking
his meals in a saddle for about sixty-three years, and the bay
horse could run. Run is not a felicitous word—he flew. And
I was rendered mentally deranged for the moment to see
that hundred paces between the bay and Spot materially
lessen at every jump. Spot lengthened out, seemed to go
down near the ground, and cut the air like a highgeared
auto. If I had not heard the fast rhythmic beat of his hoofs,
and had not bounced high into the air at every jump, I
would have been sure I was riding a bird. I tried to stop
him. As well might I have tried to pull in the *Lusitania* with
a thread. Spot was out to overhaul that bay, and in spite of
me, he was doing it. The wind rushed into my face and sang
in my ears. Jones seemed the nucleus of a sort of haze, and
he grew larger and larger. Presently he became clearly
defined in my sight; the violent commotion under me
subsided; I once more felt the saddle, and then I realized
that Spot had been content to stop alongside of Jones,
tossing his head and champing his bit.

"Well, by George! I didn't know you were in the
stretch," cried my companion. "That was a fine little brush.
We must have come several miles. I'd have killed those
wolves if I'd brought a gun. The big one that had the calf
was a bold brute. He never let go until I was within fifty
feet of him. Then I almost rode him down. I don't think the
calf was much hurt. But those blood-thirsty devils will
return, and like as not get the calf. That's the worst of cattle
raising. Now, take the buffalo. Do you suppose those
wolves could have gotten a buffalo calf out from under the
mother? Never. Neither could a whole band of wolves.
Buffalo stick close together, and the little ones do not stray.

When danger threatens, the herd closes in and faces it and fights. That is what is grand about the buffalo and what made them once roam the prairies in countless, endless droves."

From the highest elevation in that part of the range we viewed the surrounding ridges, flats and hollows, searching for the buffalo. At length we spied a cloud of dust rising from behind an undulating mound, then big black dots hove in sight.

"Frank has rounded up the herd, and is driving it this way. We'll wait," said Jones.

Though the buffalo appeared to be moving fast, a long time elapsed before they reached the foot of our outlook. They lumbered along in a compact mass, so dense that I could not count them, but I estimated the number at seventy-five. Frank was riding zigzag behind them, swinging his lariat and yelling. When he espied us he reined in his horse and waited. Then the herd slowed down, halted and began browsing.

"Look at the cattalo calves," cried Jones, in ecstatic tones. "See how shy they are, how close they stick to their mothers."

The little dark-brown fellows were plainly frightened. I made several unsuccessful attempts to photograph them, and gave it up when Jones told me not to ride too close and that it would be better to wait till we had them in the corral.

He took my camera and instructed me to go on ahead, in the rear of the herd. I heard the click of the instrument as he snapped a picture, and then suddenly heard him shout in alarm: "Look out! look out! pull your horse!"

Thundering hoof-beats pounding the earth accompanied his words. I saw a big bull, with head down, tail raised, charging my horse. He answered Frank's yell of command with a furious grunt. I was paralyzed at the wonderfully swift action of the shaggy brute, and I sat helpless. Spot wheeled as if he were on a pivot and plunged out of the way with a celerity that was astounding. The buffalo stopped, pawed the ground, and angrily tossed his huge head. Frank rode up to him, yelled, and struck him with the lariat, whereupon he gave another toss of his horns, and then returned to the herd.

"It was that darned white nag," said Jones. "Frank, it was wrong to put an inexperienced man on Spot. For that matter, the horse should never be allowed to go near the buffalo."

"Spot knows the buffs; they'd never get to him," replied Frank. But the usual spirit was absent from his voice, and he glanced at me soberly. I knew I had turned white, for I felt the peculiar cold sensation in my face.

"Now, look at that, will you?" cried Jones. "I don't like the looks of that."

He pointed to the herd. They stopped browsing, and were uneasily shifting to and fro. The bull lifted his head; the others slowly grouped together.

"Storm! Sandstorm!" exclaimed Jones, pointing desertward. Dark yellow clouds like smoke were rolling, sweeping, bearing down upon us. They expanded, blossoming out like gigantic roses, and whirled and merged into one another, all the time rolling on and blotting out the light.

"We've got to run. That storm may last two days," yelled Frank to me. "We've had some bad ones lately. Give your horse free rein, and cover your face."

A roar, resembling an approaching storm at sea, came on puffs of wind, as the horse got into their stride. Long streaks of dust whipped up in different places; the silver-white grass bent to the ground; round bunches of sage went rolling before us. The puffs grew longer, steadier, harder. Then a shrieking blast howled on our trail, seeming to swoop down on us with a yellow, blinding pall. I shut my eyes and covered my face with a handkerchief. The sand blew so thick that it filled my gloves, pebbles struck me hard enough to sting through my coat.

Fortunately, Spot kept to an easy swinging lope, which was the most comfortable motion for me. But I began to get numb, and could hardly stick on the saddle. Almost before I had dared to hope, Spot stopped. Uncovering my face, I saw Jim in the doorway of the lee side of the cabin. The yellow, streaky, whistling clouds of sand split on the cabin and passed on, leaving a small, dusty space of light.

"Shore Spot do hate to be beat," yelled Jim, as he helped me off. I stumbled into the cabin and fell upon a buffalo robe and lay there absolutely spent. Jones and Frank came in a few minutes apart, each anathematizing the gritty, powdery sand.

All day the desert storm raged and roared. The dust sifted through the numerous cracks in the cabin, burdened our clothes, spoiled our food and blinded our eyes. Wind, snow, sleet and rainstorms are discomforting enough under trying circumstances; but all combined, they are nothing to the choking, stinging, blinding sandstorm.

"Shore it'll let up by sundown," averred Jim. And sure enough the roar died away about five o'clock, the wind abated and the sand settled.

Just before supper, a knock sounded heavily on the cabin door. Jim opened it to admit one of Emmett's sons and a very tall man whom none of us knew. He was a sand-man. All that was not sand seemed a space or two of corduroy, a big bone-handled knife, a prominent square jaw and bronzed cheek and flashing eyes.

"Get down—get down, an' come in, stranger," said Frank cordially.

"How do you do, sir," said Jones.

"Colonel Jones, I've been on your trail for twelve days," announced the stranger, with a grim smile. The sand streamed off his coat in little white streaks.

Jones appeared to be casting about in his mind.

"I'm Grant Wallace," continued the newcomer. "I missed you at the El Tovar, at Williams and at Flagstaff, where I was one day behind. Was half a day late at the Little Colorado, saw your train cross Moncaupie Wash, and missed you because of the sandstorm there. Saw you from the other side of the Big Colorado as you rode out from Emmett's along the red wall. And here I am. We've never met till now, which obviously isn't my fault."

The Colonel and I fell upon Wallace's neck. Frank manifested his usual alert excitation, and said: "Well, I guess he won't hang fire on a long cougar chase." And Jim—slow, careful Jim, dropped a plate with the exclamation: "Shore it do beat hell!" The hounds sniffed round Wallace, and welcomed him with vigorous tails.

Supper that night, even if we did grind sand with our

teeth, was a joyous occasion. The biscuits were flaky and light; the bacon fragrant and crisp. I produced a jar of blackberry jam, which by subtle cunning I had been able to secrete from the Mormons on that dry desert ride, and it was greeted with acclamations of pleasure. Wallace, divested of his sand guise, beamed with the gratification of a hungry man once more in the presence of friends and food. He made large cavities in Jim's great pot of potato stew, and caused biscuits to vanish in a way that would not have shamed a Hindoo magician. The grand cañon he dug in my jar of jam, however, could not have been accomplished by legerdemain.

Talk became animated on dogs, cougars, horses and buffalo. Jones told of our experience out on the range, and concluded with some salient remarks.

"A tame wild animal is the most dangerous of beasts. My old friend, Dick Rock, a great hunter and guide out of Idaho, laughed at my advice, and got killed by one of his three-year-old bulls. I told him they knew him just well enough to kill him, and they did. My friend, A. H. Cole, of Oxford, Nebraska, tried to rope a Weetah that was too tame to be safe, and the bull killed him. Same with General Bull, a member of the Kansas Legislature, and two cowboys who went into a corral to tie up a tame elk at the wrong time. I pleaded with them not to undertake it. They had not studied animals as I had. That tame elk killed all of them. He had to be shot in order to get General Bull off his great antlers. You see, a wild animal must learn to respect a man. The way I used to teach the Yellowstone Park bears to be respectful and safe neighbors was to rope them around the front paw, swing them up on a tree clear of the ground, and whip them with a long pole. It was a dangerous business, and looks cruel, but it is the only way I could find to make the bears good. You see, they eat scraps around the hotels and get so tame they will steal everything but red-hot stoves, and will cuff the life out of those who try to shoo them off. But after a bear mother has had a licking, she not only becomes a good bear for the rest of her life, but she tells all her cubs about it with a good smack of her paw, for emphasis, and teaches them to respect peaceable citizens generation after generation.

"One of the hardest jobs I ever tackled was that of supplying the buffalo for Bronx Park. I rounded up a magnificent 'king' buffalo bull, belligerent enough to fight a battleship. When I rode after him the cowmen said I was as good as killed. I made a lance by driving a nail into the end of a short pole and sharpening it. After he had chased me, I wheeled my broncho, and hurled the lance into his back, ripping a wound as long as my hand. That put the fear of Providence into him and took the fight all out of him. I drove him uphill and down, and across cañons at a dead run for eight miles single-handed, and loaded him on a freight car; but he came near getting me once or twice, and only quick broncho work and lance play saved me.

"In the Yellowstone Park all our buffaloes have become docile, excepting the huge bull which led them. The Indians call the buffalo leader the 'Weetah,' the master of the herd. It was sure death to go near this one. So I shipped in another Weetah, hoping that he might whip some of the fight out of old Manitou, the Mighty. They came together head on, like a railway collision, and ripped up over a square mile of landscape, fighting till night came on, and then on into the night.

"I jumped into the field with them, chasing them with my biograph, getting a series of moving pictures of that bullfight which was sure the real thing. It was a ticklish thing to do, though knowing that neither bull dared take his eyes off his adversary for a second, I felt reasonably safe. The old Weetah beat the new champion out that night, but the next morning they were at it again, and the new buffalo finally whipped the old one into submission. Since then his spirit has remained broken, and even a child can approach him safely—but the new Weetah is in turn a holy terror.

"To handle buffalo, elk and bear, you must get into sympathy with their methods of reasoning. No tenderfoot stands any show, even with the tame animals of the Yellowstone."

The old buffalo hunter's lips were no longer locked. One after another he told reminiscences of his eventful life, in a simple manner; yet so vivid and gripping were the unvarnished details that I was spellbound.

"Considering what appears the impossibility of capturing a full-grown buffalo, how did you earn the name of preserver of the American bison?" inquired Wallace.

"It took years to learn how, and ten more to capture the fifty-eight that I was able to keep. I tried every plan under the sun. I roped hundreds, of all sizes and ages. They would not live in captivity. If they could not find an embankment over which to break their necks, they would crash their skulls on stones. Failing any means like that, they would lie down, will themselves to die, and die. Think of a savage wild nature that could will its heart to cease beating! But it's true. Finally I found I could keep only calves under three months of age. But to capture them so young entailed time and patience. For the buffalo fight for their young, and when I say fight, I mean till they drop. I almost always had to go alone, because I could neither coax nor hire any one to undertake it with me. Sometimes I would be weeks getting one calf. One day I captured eight—eight little buffalo calves! Never will I forget that day as long as I live!"

"Tell us about it," I suggested, in a matter of fact, round-the-campfire voice. Had the silent plainsman ever told a complete and full story of his adventures? I doubted it. He was not the man to eulogize himself.

A short silence ensued. The cabin was snug and warm; the ruddy embers glowed; one of Jim's pots steamed musically and fragrantly. The hounds lay curled in the cozy chimney corner.

Jones began to talk again, simply and unaffectedly, of his famous exploit; and as he went on so modestly, passing lightly over features we recognized as wonderful, I allowed the fire of my imagination to fuse for myself all the toil, patience, endurance, skill, herculean strength and marvelous courage and unfathomable passion which he slighted in his narrative.

3

The Last Herd

Over gray No-Man's-Land stole down the shadows of night. The undulating prairie shaded dark to the western horizon, rimmed with a fading streak of light. Tall figures, silhouetted sharply against the last golden glow of sunset, marked the rounded crest of a grassy knoll.

"Wild hunter!" cried a voice in sullen rage, "buffalo or no, we halt here. Did Adams and I hire to cross the Staked Plains? Two weeks in No-Man's-Land, and now we're facing the sand! We've one keg of water, yet you want to keep on. Why, man, you're crazy! You didn't tell us you wanted buffalo alive. And here you've got us looking death in the eye!"

In the grim silence that ensued the two men unhitched the team from the long, light wagon, while the buffalo hunter staked out his wiry, lithe-limbed racehorses. Soon a fluttering blaze threw a circle of light, which shone on the agitated face of Rude and Adams, and the cold, iron-set visage of their brawny leader.

"It's this way," began Jones, in slow, cool voice: "I engaged you fellows, and you promised to stick by me. We've had no luck. But I've finally found sign—old sign, I'll admit—of the buffalo I'm looking for—the last herd on the plains. For two years I've been hunting this herd. So have other hunters. Millions of buffalo have been killed and left to rot. Soon this herd will be gone, and then the only

32

buffalo in the world will be those I have given ten years of the hardest work in capturing. This is the last herd, I say, and my last chance to capture a calf or two. Do you imagine I'd quit? You fellows go back if you want, but I keep on."

"We can't go back. We're lost. We'll have to go with you. But, man, thirst is not the only risk we run. This is Comanche country. And if that herd is in here the Indians have it spotted."

"That worries me some," replied the plainsman, "but we'll keep on."

They slept. The night wind swished the grasses; dark storm clouds blotted out the northern stars; the prairie wolves mourned dismally.

Day broke cold, wan, threatening, under a leaden sky. The hunters traveled thirty miles by noon, and halted in a hollow where a stream flowed in wet season. Cottonwood trees were bursting into green; thickets of prickly thorn, dense and matted, showed bright spring buds.

"What is it?" suddenly whispered Rude.

The plainsman lay in strained posture, his ear against the ground.

"Hide the wagon and horses in the clump of cotton-woods," he ordered, tersely. Springing to his feet, he ran to the top of the knoll above the hollow, where he again placed his ear to the ground.

Jones's practiced ear had detected the quavering rumble of far-away, thundering hoofs. He searched the wide waste of plain with his powerful glass. To the southwest, miles distant, a cloud of dust mushroomed skyward. "Not buffalo," he muttered, "maybe wild horses." He watched and waited. The yellow cloud rolled forward, enlarging, spreading out, and drove before it a darkly indistinct, moving mass. As soon as he had one good look at this he ran back to his comrades.

"Stampede! Wild horses! Indians! Look to your rifles and hide!"

Wordless and pale, the men examined their Sharps, and made ready to follow Jones. He slipped into the thorny brake and, flat on his stomach, wormed his way like a snake far into the thickly interlaced web of branches. Rude and

Adams crawled after him. Words were superfluous. Quiet, breathless, with beating hearts, the hunters pressed close to the dry grass. A long, low, steady rumble filled the air, and increased in volume till it became a roar. Moments, endless moments, passed. The roar filled out like a flood slowly released from its confines to sweep down with the sound of doom. The ground began to tremble and quake: the light faded; the smell of dust pervaded the thicket, then a continuous streaming roar, deafening as persistent roll of thunder, pervaded the hiding place. The stampeding horses had split round the hollow. The roar lessened. Swiftly as a departing snow-squall rushing on through the pines, the thunderous thud and tramp of hoofs died away.

The trained horses hidden in the cottonwoods never stirred. "Lie low! lie low!" breathed the plainsman to his companions.

Throb of hoofs again became audible, not loud and madly pounding as those that had passed, but low, muffled, rhythmic. Jones's sharp eye, through a peephole in the thicket, saw a cream-colored mustang bob over the knoll, carrying an Indian. Another and another, then a swiftly following, close-packed throng appeared. Bright red feathers and white gleamed; weapons glinted; gaunt, bronzed savages leaned forward on racy, slender mustangs.

The plainsman shrank closer to the ground. "Apache!" he exclaimed to himself, and gripped his rifle. The band galloped down to the hollow, and slowing up, piled single file over the bank. The leader, a short, squat chief, plunged into the brake not twenty yards from the hidden men. Jones recognized the cream mustang; he knew the somber, sinister, broad face. It belonged to the Red Chief of the Apaches.

"Geronimo!" murmured the plainsman through his teeth.

Well for the Apache that no falcon savage eye discovered aught strange in the little hollow! One look at the sand of the stream bed would have cost him his life. But the Indians crossed the thicket too far up; they cantered up the slope and disappeared. The hoof-beats softened and ceased.

"Gone?" whispered Rude.

"Gone. But wait," whispered Jones. He knew the savage nature, and he knew how to wait. After a long time, he cautiously crawled out of the thicket and searched the surroundings with a plainsman's eye. He climbed the slope and saw the clouds of dust, the near one small, the far one large, which told him all he needed to know.

"Comanches?" queried Adams, with a quaver in his voice. He was new to the plains.

"Likely," said Jones, who thought it best not to tell all he knew. Then he added to himself: "We've no time to lose. There's water back here somewhere. The Indians have spotted the buffalo, and were running the horses away from the water."

The three got under way again, proceeding carefully, so as not to raise the dust, and headed due southwest. Scantier and scantier grew the grass; the hollows were washes of sand; steely gray dunes, like long, flat, ocean swells, ribbed the prairie. The gray day declined. Late into the purple night they traveled, then camped without fire.

In the gray morning Jones climbed a high ride and scanned the southwest. Low dun-colored sandhills waved from him down and down, in slow, deceptive descent. A solitary and remote waste reached out into gray infinitude. A pale lake, gray as the rest of that gray expanse, glimmered in the distance.

"Mirage!" he muttered, focusing his glass, which only magnified all under the dead gray, steely sky. "Water must be somewhere; but can that be it? It's too pale and elusive to be real. No life—a blasted, staked plain! Hello!"

A thin, black, wavering line of wild fowl, moving in beautiful, rapid flight, crossed the line of his vision. "Geese flying north, and low. There's water here," he said. He followed the flock with his glass, saw them circle over the lake, and vanish in the gray sheen.

"It's water." He hurried back to camp. His haggard and worn companions scorned his discovery. Adams siding with Rude, who knew the plains, said: "Mirage! the lure of the desert!" Yet dominated by a force too powerful for them to resist, they followed the buffalo-hunter. All day the gleaming lake beckoned them onward, and seemed to recede. All day the drab clouds scudded before the cold north wind. In the gray twilight, the lake suddenly lay before them, as if it had opened at their feet. The men rejoiced, the horses lifted their noses and sniffed the damp air.

The whinnies of the horses, the clank of harness, and splash of water, the whirr of ducks did not blur out of Jones's keen ear a sound that made him jump. It was the thump of hoofs, in a familiar beat, beat, beat. He saw a shadow moving up a ridge. Soon, outlined black against the yet light sky, a lone buffalo cow stood like a statue. A moment she held toward the lake, studying the danger, then went out of sight over the ridge.

Jones spurred his horse up the ascent, which was rather long and steep, but he mounted the summit in time to see the cow join eight huge, shaggy buffalo. The hunter reined in his horse, and standing high in his stirrups, held his hat at arms' length over his head. So he thrilled to a moment he had sought for two years. The last herd of American bison was near at hand. The cow would not venture far from the main herd; the eight stragglers were the old broken-down bulls that had been expelled, at this season, from the herd by younger and more vigorous bulls. The old monarchs saw the hunter at the same time his eyes were gladdened by sight of them, and lumbered away after the cow, to disappear in the gathering darkness. Frightened buffalo always make straight for their fellows; and this knowledge contented Jones to return to the lake, well satisfied that the herd would not be far away in the morning, within easy striking distance by daylight.

At dark the storm which had threatened for days, broke in a fury of rain, sleet and hail. The hunters stretched a piece of canvas over the wheels of the north side of the wagon, and wet and shivering, crawled under it to their blankets. During the night the storm raged with unabated strength.

Dawn, forbidding and raw, lightened to the whistle of the sleety gusts. Fire was out of the question. Chary of weight, the hunters had carried no wood, and the buffalo chips they used for fuel were lumps of ice. Grumbling, Adams and Rude ate a cold breakfast, while Jones, munching a biscuit, faced the biting blast from the crest of the ridge. The middle of the plain below held a ragged, circular mass, as still as stone. It was the buffalo herd, with every shaggy head to the storm. So they would stand, never budging from their tracks, till the blizzard of sleet was over.

Jones, though eager and impatient, restrained himself, for it was unwise to begin operations in the storm. There was nothing to do but wait. Ill fared the hunters that day. Food had to be eaten uncooked. The long hours dragged by with the little group huddled under icy blankets. When darkness fell, the sleet changed to drizzling rain. This blew over at midnight, and a colder wind, penetrating to the very marrow of the sleepless men, made their condition worse. In the after part of the night, the wolves howled mournfully.

With a gray, misty light appearing in the east, Jones threw off his stiff, ice-incased blanket, and crawled out. A gaunt gray wolf, the color of the day and the sand and the lake, sneaked away, looking back. While moving and threshing about to warm his frozen blood, Jones munched another biscuit. His men crawled from under the wagon, and made an unfruitful search for the whisky. Fearing it, Jones had thrown the bottle away. The men cursed. The patient horses drooped sadly, and shivered in the lee of the improvised tent. Jones kicked the inch-thick casing of ice from his saddle. Kentuck, his racer, had been spared on the whole trip for this day's work. The thoroughbred was cold, but as Jones threw the saddle over him, he showed that he knew the chase ahead, and was eager to be off. At last, after repeated efforts with his benumbed fingers, Jones got the girths tight. He tied a bunch of soft cords to the saddle and mounted.

"Follow as fast as you can," he called to his surly men. "The buffs will run north against the wind. This is the right direction for us; we'll soon leave the sand. Stick to my trail and come a-humming."

From the ridge he met the red sun, rising bright, and a keen northeasterly wind that lashed like a whip. As he had anticipated, his quarry had moved northward. Kentuck let out into a swinging stride, which in an hour had the loping herd in sight. Every jump now took him upon higher ground, where the sand failed, and the grass grew thicker and began to bend under the wind.

In the teeth of the nipping gale Jones slipped close upon the herd without alarming even a cow. More than a hundred little reddish-black calves leisurely loped in the rear. Kentuck, keen to his work, crept on like a wolf, and the hunter's great fist clenched the coiled lasso. Before him expanded a boundless plain. A situation long cherished and dreamed of had become a reality. Kentuck, fresh and strong, was good for all day. Jones gloated over the little red bulls and heifers, as a miser gloats over gold and jewels. Never before had he caught more than two in one day, and often it had taken days to capture one. This was the last herd, this the last opportunity toward perpetuating a grand race of beasts. And with born instinct he saw ahead the day of his life.

At a touch, Kentuck closed in, and the buffalo, seeing him, stampeded into the heaving roll so well known to the hunter. Racing on the right flank of the herd, Jones selected a tawny heifer and shot the lariat after her. It fell true, but being stiff and kinky from the sleet, failed to tighten, and the quick calf leaped through the loop to freedom.

Undismayed the pursuer quickly recovered his rope. Again he whirled and sent the loop. Again it circled true, and failed to close; again the agile heifer bounded through it. Jones whipped the air with the stubborn rope. To lose a chance like that was worse than boy's work.

The third whirl, running a smaller loop, tightened the coil round the frightened calf just back of its ears. A pull on the bridle brought Kentuck to a halt in his tracks, and the baby buffalo rolled over and over in the grass. Jones bounced from his seat and jerked loose a couple of the soft cords. In a twinkling his big knee crushed down on the calf, and his big hands bound it helpless.

Kentuck neighed. Jones saw his black ears go up. Danger threatened. For a moment the hunter's blood turned chill, not from fear, for he never felt fear, but because he thought the Indians were returning to ruin his work. His eye swept the plain. Only the gray forms of wolves flitted through the grass, here, there, all about him. Wolves! They were as fatal to his enterprise as savages. A trooping pack of prairie wolves had fallen in with the herd and hung close on the trail, trying to cut a calf away from its mother. The gray brutes boldly trotted to within a few yards of him, and slyly looked at him, with pale, fiery eyes. They had already scented his captive. Precious time flew by; the situation, critical and baffling, had never before been met by him. There lay his little calf tied fast, and to the north ran many others, some of which he must—he would have. To think quickly had meant the solving of many a plainsman's problem. Should he stay with his prize to save it, or leave it to be devoured?

"Ha! you old gray devils!" he yelled, shaking his fist at the wolves. "I know a trick or two." Slipping his hat between the legs of the calf, he fastened it securely. This done, he vaulted on Kentuck, and was off with never a backward glance. Certain it was that the wolves would not touch anything, alive or dead, that bore the scent of a human being.

The bison scoured away a long half-mile in the lead, sailing northward like a cloud-shadow over the plain. Kentuck, mettlesome, over-eager, would have run himself out in short order, but the wary hunter, strong to restrain as well as impel, with the long day in his mind, kept the steed in his easy stride, which, springy and stretching, over-hauled the herd in the course of several miles.

A dash, a whirl, a shock, a leap, horse and hunter working in perfect accord, and a fine big calf, bellowing lustily, struggled desperately for freedom under the re-morseless knee. The big hands toyed with him; and then, secure in the double knots, the calf lay still, sticking out his tongue and rolling his eyes, with the coat of the hunter tucked under his bonds to keep away the wolves.

The race had but begun; the horse had but warmed to his work; the hunter had but tasted of sweep triumph. Another hopeful of a buffalo mother, negligent in danger, truant from his brothers, stumbled and fell in the enmesh-ing loop. The hunter's vest, slipped over the calf's neck, served as danger signal to the wolves. Before the lumbering buffalo missed their loss, another red and black baby kicked helplessly on the grass and sent up vain, weak calls, and at last lay still, with the hunter's boot tied to his cords.

Four! Jones counted them aloud, and in his mind, and kept on! Fast, hard work, covering upward of fifteen miles, had begun to tell on herd, horse and man, and all slowed down to the call for strength. The fifth time Jones closed in on his game, he encountered different circumstances such as called forth his cunning.

The herd had opened up; the mothers had fallen back to the rear; the calves hung almost out of sight under the shaggy sides of protectors. To try them out Jones darted close and threw his lasso. It struck a cow. With activity incredible in such a huge beast, she lunged at him. Kentuck, expecting just such a move, wheeled to safety. This duel, ineffectual on both sides, kept up for a while, and all the time, man and herd were jogging rapidly to the north.

Jones could not let well enough alone; he acknowledged this even as he swore he must have five. Emboldened by his marvelous luck, and yielding headlong to the passion within, he threw caution to the winds. A lame old cow with a red calf caught his eye; in he spurred his willing horse and slung his rope. It stung the haunch of the mother. The mad grunt she vented was no quicker than the velocity with which she plunged and reared. Jones had but time to swing his leg over the saddle when the hoofs beat down. Kentuck rolled on the plain, flinging his rider from him. The infuriated buffalo lowered her head for the fatal charge on the horse, when the plainsman, jerking out his heavy Colts, shot her dead in her tracks.

Kentuck got to his feet unhurt, and stood his ground, quivering but ready, showing his steadfast courage. He showed more, for his ears lay back, and his eyes had the gleam of the animal that strikes back.

The calf ran round its mother. Jones lassoed it, and tied it down, being compelled to cut a piece from his lasso, as the cords on the saddle had given out. He left his other boot with baby number five. The still heaving, smoking body of the victim called forth the stern, intrepid hunter's pity for a moment. Spill of blood he had not wanted. But he had not been able to avoid it; and mounting again with close-shut jaw and smoldering eye, he galloped to the north.

Kentuck snorted; the pursuing wolves shied off in the grass; the pale sun began to slant westward. The cold iron stirrups froze and cut the hunter's bootless feet.

When once more he came hounding the buffalo, they were considerably winded. Short-tufted tails, raised stiffly, gave warning. Snorts, like puffs of escaping steam, and deep grunts from cavernous chests evinced anger and impatience that might, at any moment, bring the herd to a defiant stand.

He whizzed the shortened noose over the head of a calf that was laboring painfully to keep up, and had slipped down, when a mighty grunt told him of peril. Never looking to see whence it came, he sprang into the saddle. Fiery Kentuck jumped into action, then hauled up with a shock that almost threw himself and rider. The lasso, fast to the horse, and its loop end round the calf, had caused the sudden check.

A maddened cow bore down on Kentuck. The gallant horse straightened in a jump, but dragging the calf pulled him in a circle, and in another moment he was running round and round the howling, kicking pivot. Then ensued a terrible race, with horse and bison describing a twenty-foot circle. Bang! Bang! The hunter fired two shots, and heard the spats of the bullets. But they only augmented the frenzy of the beast. Faster Kentuck flew, snorting in terror; closer drew the dusty, bouncing pursuer; the calf spun like a top; the lasso strung tighter than wire. Jones strained to loosen the fastening, but in vain. He swore at his carelessness in dropping his knife by the last calf he had tied. He thought of shooting the rope, yet dared not risk the shot. A hollow sound turned him again, with the Colts leveled. Bang! Dust flew from the ground beyond the bison.

The two charges left in the gun were all that stood between him and eternity. With a desperate display of strength Jones threw his weight in a backward pull, and hauled Kentuck up. Then he leaned far back in the saddle, and shoved the Colts out beyond the horse's flank. Down went the broad head, with its black, glistening horns. Bang! She slid forward with a crash, plowing the ground with hoofs and nose—spouted blood, uttered a hoarse cry, kicked and died.

Kentuck, for once completely terrorized, reared and plunged from the cow, dragging the calf. Stern command and iron arm forced him to a standstill. The calf, nearly strangled, recovered when the noose was slipped, and moaned a feeble protest against life and captivity. The remainder of Jones's lasso went to bind number six, and one of his socks went to serve as reminder to the persistent wolves.

"Six! On! On! Kentuck! On!" Weakening, but unconscious of it, with bloody hands and feet, without lasso, and with only one charge in his revolver, hatless, coatless, vestless, bootless, the wild hunter urged on the noble horse. The herd had gained miles in the interval of the fight. Game to the backbone, Kentuck lengthened out to overhaul it, and slowly the rolling gap lessened and lessened. A long hour thumped away, with the rumble growing nearer.

Once again the lagging calves dotted the grassy plain before the hunter. He dashed beside a burly calf, grasped its tail, stopped his horse, and jumped. The calf went down with him, and did not come up. The knotted, blood-stained hands, like claws of steel, bound the hind legs close and fast with a leathern belt, and left between them a torn and bloody sock.

"Seven! On! Old Faithful! We *must* have another! the last! This is your day."

The blood that flecked the hunter was not all his own.

The sun slanted westwardly toward the purpling horizon; the grassy plain gleamed like a ruffled sea of glass; the gray wolves loped on.

When next the hunger came within sight of the herd, over a wavy ridge, changes in its shape and movement met his gaze. The calves were almost done; they could run no more; their mothers faced the south, and trotted slowly to and fro; the bulls were grunting, herding, piling close. It looked as if the herd meant to stand and fight.

This mattered little to the hunter who had captured seven calves since dawn. The first limping calf he reached tried to elude the grasping hand and failed. Kentuck had been trained to wheel to the right or left, in whichever way his rider leaned; and as Jones bent over and caught an upraised tail, the horse turned to strike the calf with both front hoofs. The calf rolled; the horse plunged down; the rider sped beyond to the dust. Though the calf was tired, he still could bellow, and he filled the air with robust bawls.

Jones all at once saw twenty or more buffalo dash in at him with fast, twinkling, short legs. With the thought of it, he was in the air to the saddle. As the black, round mounds charged from every direction, Kentuck let out with all there was left in him. He leaped and whirled, pitched and swerved, in a roaring, clashing, dusty mêlée. Beating hoofs threw the turf, flying tails whipped the air, and everywhere were dusky, sharp-pointed heads, tossing low. Kentuck squeezed out unscathed. The mob of bison, bristling, turned to lumber after the main herd. Jones seized his opportunity and rode after them, yelling with all his might. He drove them so hard that soon the little fellows lagged paces behind. Only one or two old cows straggled with the calves.

Then wheeling Kentuck, he cut between the herd and a calf, and rode it down. Bewildered, the tously little bull bellowed in great affright. The hunter seized the stiff tail, and calling to his horse, leaped off. But his strength was far spent, and the buffalo, larger than his fellows, threshed about and jerked in terror. Jones threw it again and again. But it struggled up, never once ceasing its loud demands for help. Finally the hunter tripped it up and fell upon it with his knees.

Above the rumble of retreating hoofs, Jones heard the familiar short, quick, jarring pound on the turf. Kentuck neighed his alarm and raced to the right. Bearing down on the hunter, hurtling through the air, was a giant furry mass, instinct with fierce life and power—a buffalo cow robbed of her young.

With his senses almost numb, barely able to pull and raise the Colt, the plainsman willed to live, and to keep his captive. His leveled arm wavered like a leaf in a storm.

Bang! Fire, smoke, a shock, a jarring crash, and silence!

The calf stirred beneath him. He put out a hand to touch a warm, furry coat. The mother had fallen beside him. Lifting a heavy hoof, he laid it over the neck of the calf to serve as additional weight. He lay still and listened. The rumble of the herd died away in the distance.

The evening waned. Still the hunter lay quiet. From time to time the calf struggled and bellowed. Lank, gray wolves appeared on all sides; they prowled about with hungry howls, and shoved black-tipped noses through the grass. The sun sank, and the sky paled to opal blue. A star shone out, then another, and another. Over the prairie slanted the first dark shadow of night.

Suddenly the hunter laid his ear to the ground, and listened. Faint beats, like throbs of a pulsing heart, shuddered from the soft turf. Stronger they grew, till the hunter raised his head. Dark forms approached, voices broke the silence; the creaking of a wagon scared away the wolves.

"This way!" shouted the hunter weakly.

"Ha! here he is. Hurt?" cried Rude, vaulting the wheel.

"Tie up this calf. How many—did you find?" The voice grew fainter.

"Seven—alive, and in good shape, and all your clothes."

But the last words fell on unconscious ears.

4

The Trail

"Frank, what'll we do about horses?" asked Jones. "Jim'll want the bay, and of course you'll want to ride Spot. The rest of our nags will only do to pack the outfit."

"I've been thinkin'," replied the foreman. "You sure will need good mounts. Now it happens that a friend of mine is just at this time at House Rock Valley, an outlyin' post of one of the big Utah ranches. He is gettin' in the horses off the range, an' he has some crackin' good ones. Let's ooze over there—it's only thirty miles—an' get some horses from him."

We were all eager to act upon Frank's suggestion. So plans were made for three of us to ride over and select our mounts. Frank and Jim would follow with the pack train, and if all went well, on the following evening we would camp under the shadow of Buckskin.

Early next morning we were on our way. I tried to find a soft place on Old Baldy, one of Frank's pack horses. He was a horse that would not have raised up at the trumpet of doom. Nothing under the sun, Frank said, bothered Old Baldy but the operation of shoeing. We made the distance to the outpost by noon, and found Frank's friend a genial and obliging cowboy, who said we could have all the horses we wanted.

While Jones and Wallace strutted round the big corral, which was full of vicious, dusty, shaggy horses and mustangs, I sat high on the fence. I heard them talking about points and girth and stride, and a lot of terms that I could not understand. Wallace selected a heavy sorrel, and Jones a big bay, very like Jim's. I had observed, way over in the corner of the corral, a bunch of cayuses, and among them a clean-limbed black horse. Edging round on the fence I got a closer view, and then cried out that I had found my horse. I jumped down and caught him, much to my surprise, for the other horses were wild, and had kicked viciously. The black was beautifully built, wide-chested and powerful, but not heavy. His coat glistened like sheeny black satin, and he had a white face and white feet and a long mane.

"I don't know about giving you Satan—that's his name," said the cowboy. "The foreman rides him often. He's the fastest, the best climber, and the best dispositioned horse on the range.

"But I guess I can let you have him," he continued, when he saw my disappointed face.

"By George!" exclaimed Jones. "You've got it on us this time."

"Would you like to trade?" asked Wallace, as his sorrel tried to bite him. "That black looks sort of fierce."

I led my prize out of the corral, up to the little cabin nearby, where I tied him, and proceeded to get acquainted after a fashion of my own. Though not versed in horse-lore, I knew that half the battle was to win his confidence. I smoothed his silky coat, and patted him, and then surreptitiously slipped a lump of sugar from my pocket. This sugar, which I had purloined in Flagstaff, and carried all the way across the desert, was somewhat disreputably soiled, and Satan sniffed at it disdainfully. Evidently he had never smelled or tasted sugar. I pressed it into his mouth. He munched it, and then looked me over with some interest. I handed him another lump. He took it and rubbed his nose against me. Satan was mine!

Frank and Jim came along early in the afternoon. What with packing, changing saddles and shoeing the horses, we were all busy. Old Baldy would not be shod, so we let him off till a more opportune time. By four o'clock we were riding toward the slopes of Buckskin, now only a few miles away, standing up higher and darker.

"What's that for?" inquired Wallace, pointing to a long, rusty, wire-wrapped, double-barreled blunderbuss of a shotgun, stuck in the holster of Jones's saddle.

The Colonel, who had been having a fine time with the impatient and curious hounds, did not vouchsafe any information on that score. But very shortly we were destined to learn the use of this incongruous firearm. I was riding in advance of Wallace, and a little behind Jones. The dogs—excepting Jude, who had been kicked and lamed—were ranging along before their master. Suddenly, right before me, I saw an immense jack-rabbit; and just then Moze and Don caught sight of it. In fact, Moze bumped his blunt nose into the rabbit. When it leaped into scared action, Moze yelped, and Don followed suit. Then they were after it in wild, clamoring pursuit. Jones let out the stentorian blast, now becoming familiar, and spurred after them. He reached over, pulled the shotgun out of the holster and fired both barrels at the jumping dogs.

I expressed my amazement in strong language, and Wallace whistled.

Don came sneaking back with his tail between his legs, and Moze, who had cowered as if stung, circled round ahead of us. Jones finally succeeded in getting him back.

"Come in hyah! You measly rabbit dogs! What do you mean chasing off that way? We're after lions. Lions! under-stand?"

Don looked thoroughly convinced of his error, but Moze, being more thick-headed, appeared mystified rather than hurt or frightened.

"What size shot do you use?" I asked.

"Number ten. They don't hurt much at seventy-five yards," replied our leader. "I use them as sort of a long arm. You see, the dogs must be made to know what we're after. Ordinary means would never do in a case like this. My idea is to break them off coyotes, wolves and deer, and when we cross a lion trail, let them go. I'll teach them sooner than you'd think. Only we must get where we can see what they're trailing. Then I can tell whether to call them back or not."

The sun was gilding the rim of the desert ramparts when we began the ascent of the foothills of Buckskin. A steep trail wound zigzag up the mountain. We led our horses, as it was a long, hard climb. From time to time, as I stopped to catch my breath, I gazed away across the growing void to the gorgeous Pink Cliffs, far above and beyond the red wall which had seemed so high, and then out toward the desert. The irregular ragged crack in the plain, apparently only a thread of broken ground, was the Grand Cañon. How unutterably remote, wild, grand was that world of red and brown, of purple pall, of vague outline!

Two thousand feet, probably, we mounted to what Frank called Little Buckskin. In the west a copper glow, ridged with lead-colored clouds, marked where the sun had set. The air was very thin and icy cold. At the first clump of piñon pines, we made dry camp. When I sat down it was as if I had been anchored. Frank solicitously remarked that I looked "sort of beat." Jim built a roaring fire and began getting supper. A snow squall came on the rushing wind. The air grew colder, and though I hugged the fire, I could not get warm. When I had satisfied my hunger, I rolled out my sleeping-bag and crept into it. I stretched my aching limbs and did not move again. Once I awoke, drowsily feeling the warmth of the fire, and I heard Frank say: "He's asleep, dead to the world!"

"He's all in," said Jones. "Riding's what did it. You know how a horse tears a man to pieces."

"Will he be able to stand it?" asked Frank, with as much solicitude as if he were my brother. "When you get out after anythin'—well, you're hell. An' think of the country we're goin' into. I know you've never seen the breaks of the Siwash, but I have, an' it's the worst an' roughest country I ever saw. Breaks after breaks, like the ridges on a washboard, headin' on the south slope of Buckskin, an' runnin' down, side by side, miles an' miles, deeper an' deeper, till they run into that awful hole. It will be a killin' trip on men, horses an' dogs. Now, Mr. Wallace,

he's been campin' an' roughin' with the Navajos for months;
he's in some kind of shape, but—"

Frank concluded his remark with a doubtful pause.

"I'm some worried, too," replied Jones. "But he would
come. He stood the desert well enough; even the Mormons
said that."

In the ensuing silence the fire sputtered, the glare
fitfully merged into dark shadows under the weird piñons,
and the wind moaned through the short branches.

"Wal," drawled a slow, soft voice, "shore I reckon
you're hollerin' too soon. Frank's measly trick puttin' him
on Spot showed me. He rode out on Spot, an' he rode in on
Spot. Shore he'll stay."

It was not all the warmth of the blankets that glowed
over me then. The voices died away dreamily, and my
eyelids dropped sleepily tight. Late in the night I sat up
suddenly, roused by some unusual disturbance. The fire
was dead; the wind swept with a rush through the piñons.
From the black darkness came the staccato chorus of
coyotes. Don barked his displeasure; Sounder made the
welkin ring, and old Moze growled low and deep, grumbling like muttered thunder. Then all was quiet, and I
slept.

Dawn, rosy red, confronted me when I opened my
eyes. Breakfast was ready; Frank was packing Old Baldy;
Jones talked to his horse as he saddled him; Wallace came
stooping his giant figure under the piñons; the dogs, eager
and soft-eyed, sat around Jim and begged. The sun peeped
over the Pink Cliffs; the desert still lay asleep, tranced in a
purple and golden-streaked mist.

"Come, come!" said Jones, in his big voice. "We're
slow; here's the sun."

"Easy, easy," replied Frank, "we've all the time there
is." ·

When Frank threw the saddle over Satan I interrupted
him and said I would care for my horse henceforward. Soon
we were under way, the horses fresh, the dogs scenting the
keen, cold air.

The trail rolled over the ridges of piñon and scrubby
pine. Occasionally we could see the black, ragged crest of

Buckskin above us. From one of these ridges I took my last long look back at the desert, and engraved on my mind a picture of the red wall, and the many-hued ocean of sand. The trail; narrow and indistinct, mounted the last slow-rising slope; the piñons failed, and the scrubby pines became abundant. At length we reached the top, and entered the great arched aisles of Buckskin Forest. The ground was flat as a table. Magnificent pine trees, far apart, with branches high and spreading, gave the eye glad welcome. Some of these monarchs were eight feet thick at the base and two hundred feet high. Here and there one lay, gaunt and prostrate, a victim of the wind. The smell of pitch pine was sweetly overpowering.

"When I went through here two weeks ago, the snow was a foot deep, an' I bogged in places," said Frank. "The sun has been oozin' round here some. I'm afraid Jones won't find any snow on this end of Buckskin."

Thirty miles of winding trail, brown and springy from its thick mat of pine needles, shaded always by the massive, seamy-barked trees, took us over the extremity of Buckskin. Then we faced down into the head of a ravine that ever grew deeper, stonier and rougher. I shifted from side to side, from leg to leg in my saddle, dismounted and hobbled before Satan, mounted again, and rode on. Jones called the dogs and complained to them of the lack of snow. Wallace sat his horse comfortably, taking long pulls at his pipe and long gazes at the shaggy sides of the ravine. Frank, energetic and tireless, kept the pack-horses in the trail. Jim jogged on silently. And so we rode down to Oak Spring.

The spring was pleasantly situated in a grove of oaks and piñons, under the shadow of three cliffs. Three ravines opened here into an oval valley. A rude cabin of rough-hewn logs stood near the spring.

"Get down, get down," sang out Frank. "We'll hang up here. Beyond Oak is No-Man's-Land. We take our chances on water after we leave here."

When we had unsaddled, unpacked, and got a fire roaring on the wide stone hearth of the cabin, it was once again night.

"Boys," said Jones after supper, "we're now on the

edge of lion country. Frank saw lion sign in here only two weeks ago; and though the snow is gone, we stand a show of finding tracks in the sand and dust. To-morrow morning, before the sun gets a chance at the bottom of these ravines, we'll be up and doing. We'll each take a dog and search in different directions. Keep the dog in leash, and when he opens up, examine the ground carefully for tracks. If a dog opens on any track that you are sure isn't a lion's, punish him. And when a lion-track is found, hold the dog in, wait and signal. We'll use a signal I have tried and found far-reaching and easy to yell. Waa-hoo! That's it. Once yelled it means come. Twice means come quickly. Three times means come—danger!"

In one corner of the cabin was a platform of poles, covered with straw. I threw the sleeping-bag on this, and was soon stretched out. Misgivings as to my strength worried me before I closed my eyes. Once on my back, I felt I could not rise; my chest was sore; my cough deep and rasping. It seemed I had scarcely closed my eyes when Jones's impatient voice recalled me from sweet oblivion.

"Frank, Frank, it's daylight. Jim—boys!" he called.

I tumbled out in a gray, wan twilight. It was cold enough to make the fire acceptable, but nothing like the morning before on Buckskin.

"Come to the festal board," drawled Jim, almost before I had my boots laced.

"Jones," said Frank, "Jim an' I'll ooze round here to-day. There's lots to do, an' we want to have things hitched right before we strike for the Siwash. We've got to shoe Old Baldy, an' if we can't get him locoed, it'll take all of us to do it."

The light was still gray when Jones led off with Don, Wallace with Sounder and I with Moze. Jones directed us to separate, follow the dry stream beds in the ravines, and remember his instructions given the night before.

The ravine to the right, which I entered, was choked with huge stones fallen from the cliff above, and piñons growing thick; and I wondered apprehensively how a man could evade a wild animal in such a place, much less chase it.

Old Moze pulled on his chain and sniffed at coyote and deer tracks. And every time he evinced interest in such, I cut him with a switch, which, to tell the truth, he did not notice.

I thought I heard a shout, and holding Moze tight, I waited and listened.

"Waa-hoo—waa-hoo!" floated on the air, rather deadened as if it had come from round the triangular cliff that faced into the valley. Urging and dragging Moze, I ran down the ravine as fast as I could, and soon encountered Wallace coming from the middle ravine.

"Jones," he said excitedly, "this way—there's the signal again."

We dashed in haste for the mouth of the third ravine, and came suddenly upon Jones, kneeling under a piñon tree.

"Boys, look!" he exclaimed, as he pointed to the ground. There, clearly defined in the dust, was a cat track as big as my spread hand, and the mere sight of it sent a chill up my spine. "There's a lion track for you; made by a female, a two-year-old; but I can't say if she passed here last night. Don won't take the trail. Try Moze."

I led Moze to the big, round imprint, and put his nose down into it. The old hound sniffed and sniffed, then lost interest.

"Cold!" ejaculated Jones. "No go. Try Sounder. Come, old boy, you've the nose for it."

He urged the reluctant hound forward. Sounder needed not to be shown the trail; he stuck his nose in it, and stood very quiet for a long moment; then he quivered slightly, raised his nose and sought the next track. Step by step he went slowly, doubtfully. All at once his tail wagged stiffly.

"Look at that!" cried Jones in delight. "He's caught a scent when the others couldn't. Hyah, Moze, get back. Keep Moze and Don back; give him room."

Slowly Sounder paced up the ravine, as carefully as if he were traveling on thin ice. He passed the dusty, open trail to a scaly ground with little bits of grass, and he kept on.

We were electrified to hear him give vent to a deep bugle-blast note of eagerness.

"By George, he's got it, boys!" exclaimed Jones, as he lifted the stubborn, struggling hound off the trail. "I know that bay. It means a lion passed here this morning. And we'll get him up as sure as you're alive. Come, Sounder. Now for the horses."

As we ran pell-mell into the little glade, where Jim sat mending some saddle trapping, Frank rode up the trail with the horses.

"Well, I heard Sounder," he said with his genial smile. "Somethin's comin' off, eh? You'll have to ooze round some to keep up with that hound."

I saddled Satan with fingers that trembled in excitement, and pushed my little Remington automatic into the rifle holster.

"Boys, listen," said our leader. "We're off now in the beginning of a hunt new to you. Remember—no shooting, no blood-letting, except in self-defense. Keep as close to me as you can. Listen for the dogs, and when you fall behind or separate, yell out the signal cry. Don't forget this. We're bound to lose each other. Look out for the spikes and branches on the trees. If the dogs split, whoever follows the one that trees the lion must wait there till the rest come up. Off now! Come, Sounder; Moze, you rascal, hyah! Come, Don, come, Puppy, and take your medicine."

Except Moze, the hounds were all trembling and running eagerly to and fro. When Sounder was loosed, he led them in a bee-line to the trail, with us cantering after. Sounder worked exactly as before, only he followed the lions tracks a little farther up the ravine before he bayed. He kept going faster and faster, occasionally letting out one deep, short yelp. The other hounds did not give tongue, but eager, excited, baffled, kept at his heels. The ravine was long, and the wash at the bottom, up which the lion had proceeded, turned and twisted round bowlders large as houses, and led through dense growths of some short, rough shrub. Now and then the lion tracks showed plainly in the sand. For five miles or more Sounder led us up the ravine, which began to contract and grow steep. The dry stream bed got to be full of thickets of poplar—tall, straight, branchless saplings, about the size of a man's arm, and growing so close we had to press them aside to let our horses through.

Presently Sounder slowed up and appeared at fault. We found him puzzling over an open, grassy patch, and after nosing it for a little while, he began skirting the edge.

"Cute dog!" declared Jones. "That Sounder will make a lion chaser. Our game has gone up here somewhere."

Sure enough, Sounder directly gave tongue from the side of the ravine. It was climb for us now. Broken shale, rocks of all dimensions, piñons down and piñons up made ascending no easy problem. We had to dismount and lead the horses, thus losing ground. Jones forged ahead and reached the top of the ravine first. When Wallace and I got up, breathing heavily, Jones and the hounds were out of sight. But Sounder kept voicing his clear call, giving us our direction. Off we flew, over ground that was still rough, but enjoyable going compared to the ravine slopes. The ridge was sparsely covered with cedar and piñon, through which, far ahead, we pretty soon spied Jones. Wallace signaled, and our leader answered twice. We caught up with him on the brink of another ravine deeper and craggier than the first, full of dead, gnarled piñon and splintered rocks.

"This gulch is the largest of the three that head in at Oak Spring," said Jones. "Boys, don't forget your direction. Always keep a feeling where camp is, always sense it every time you turn. The dogs have gone down. That lion is in here somewhere. Maybe he lives down in the high cliffs near the spring and came up here last night for a kill he's buried somewhere. Lions never travel far. Hark! Hark! There's Sounder and the rest of them! They've got the scent; they've all got it! Down, boys, down, and ride!"

With that he crashed into the cedar in a way that showed me how impervious he was to slashing branches, sharp as thorns, and steep descent and peril. Wallace's big sorrel plunged after him and the rolling stones cracked. Suffering as I was by this time, with cramp in my legs, and torturing pain, I had to choose between holding my horse in or falling off; so I chose the former and accordingly got behind.

Dead cedar and piñon trees lay everywhere, with their contorted limbs reaching out like the arms of a devil-fish. Stones blocked every opening. Making the bottom of the ravine after what seemed an interminable time, I found the tracks of Jones and Wallace. A long "Waa-hoo!" drew me on; then the mellow bay of a hound floated up the ravine. Satan made up time in the sandy stream bed, but kept me busily dodging overhanging branches. I became aware, after a succession of efforts to keep from being strung on piñons, that the sand before me was clean and trackless. Hauling Satan up sharply, I waited irresolutely and listened. Then from high up the ravine side wafted down a medley of yelps and barks.

"Waa-hoo, waa-hoo!" ringing down the slope, pealed against the cliff behind me, and sent the wild echoes flying.

Satan, of his own accord, headed up the incline. Surprised at this, I gave him free rein. How he did climb! Not long did it take me to discover that he picked out easier going than I had. Once I saw Jones crossing a ledge far above me, and I yelled our signal cry. The answer returned clear and sharp; then its echo cracked under the hollow cliff, and crossing and recrossing the ravine, it died at last far away, like the muffled peal of a bell-buoy. Again I heard the blended yelping of the hounds, and closer at hand. I saw a long, low cliff above, and decided that the hounds were running at the base of it. Another chorus of yelps, quicker, wilder than the others, drew a yell from me. Instinctively I knew the dogs had jumped game of some kind. Satan knew it as well as I, for he quickened his pace and sent the stones clattering behind him.

I gained the base of the yellow cliff, but found no tracks in the dust of ages that had crumbled in its shadow, nor did I hear the dogs. Considering how close they had seemed, this was strange. I halted and listened. Silence reigned supreme. The ragged cracks in the cliff walls could have harbored many a watching lion, and I cast an apprehensive glance into their dark confines. Then I turned my horse to get round the cliff and over the ridge. When I again

stopped, all I could hear was the thumping of my heart and
the labored panting of Satan. I came to a break in the cliff,
a steep place of weathered rock, and I put Satan to it. He
went up with a will. From the narrow saddle of the
ridge-crest I tried to take my bearings. Below me slanted
the green of piñon, with the bleached treetops standing like
spears, and uprising yellow stones. Fancying I heard a
gunshot, I leaned a straining ear against the soft breeze.
The proof came presently in the unmistakable report of
Jones's blunderbuss. It was repeated almost instantly,
giving reality to the direction, which was down the slope of
what I concluded must be the third ravine. Wondering
what was the meaning of the shots, and chagrined because
I was out of the race, but calmer in mind, I let Satan stand.

Hardly a moment elapsed before a sharp bark tingled
in my ears. It belonged to old Moze. Soon I distinguished
a rattling of stones and the sharp, metallic clicks of hoofs
striking rocks. Then into a space below me loped a beautiful
deer, so large that at first I took it for an elk. Another sharp
bark, nearer this time, told the tale of Moze's dereliction.
In a few moments he came in sight, running with his tongue
out and his head high.

"Hyah, you old gladiator! hyah! hyah!" I yelled and
yelled again. Moze passed over the saddle on the trail of the
deer, and his short bark floated back to remind me how far
he was from a lion dog.

Then I divined the meaning of the shotgun reports.
The hounds had crossed a fresher trail than that of the lion,
and our leader had discovered it. Despite a keen appreciation of Jones's task, I gave way to amusement, and
repeated Wallace's paradoxical formula: "Pet the lions and
shoot the hounds."

So I headed down the ravine, looking for a blunt, bold
crag, which I had descried from camp. I found it before
long, and profiting by past failures to judge of distance,
gave my first impression a great stretch, and then decided
that I was more than two miles from Oak.

Long after two miles had been covered, and I had
begun to associate Jim's biscuits with a certain soft seat near
a ruddy fire, I was apparently still the same distance from

my landmark crag. Suddenly a slight noise brought me to a halt. I listened intently. Only an indistinct rattling of small rocks disturbed the impressive stillness. It might have been the weathering that goes on constantly, and it might have been an animal. I inclined to the former idea till I saw Satan's ears go up. Jones had told me to watch the ears of my horse, and short as had been my acquaintance with Satan, I had learned that he always discovered things more quickly than I. So I waited patiently.

From time to time a rattling roll of pebbles, almost musical, caught my ear. It came from the base of the wall of yellow cliff that barred the summit of all those ridges. Satan threw up his head and nosed the breeze. The delicate, almost stealthy sounds, the action of my horse, the waiting drove my heart to extra work. The breeze quickened and fanned my cheek, and borne upon it came the faint and far away bay of a hound. It came again and again, each time nearer. Then on a stronger puff of wind rang the clear, deep, mellow call that had given Sounder his beautiful name. Never it seemed had I heard music so blood-stirring. Sounder was on the trail of something, and he had it headed my way. Satan heard, shot up his long ears, and tried to go ahead; but I restrained and soothed him into quiet.

Long moments I sat there, with the poignant consciousness of the wildness of the scene, of the significant rattling of the stones and of the bell-tongued hound baying incessantly, sending warm joy through my veins, the absorption in sensations new, yielding only to the hunting instinct when Satan snorted and quivered. Again the deep-toned bay rang into the silence with its stirring thrill of life. And a sharp rattling of stones just above brought another snort from Satan.

Across an open space in the piñons a gray form flashed. I leaped off Satan and knelt to get a better view under the trees. I soon made out another deer passing along the base of the cliff. Mounting again, I rode up to the cliff to wait for Sounder.

A long time I had to wait for the hound. It proved that the atmosphere was as deceiving in regard to sound as to sight. Finally Sounder came running along the wall. I got off to intercept him. The crazy fellow—he had never responded to my overtures of friendship—uttered short, sharp yelps of delight, and actually leaped into my arms. But I could not hold him. He darted upon the trail again and paid no heed to my angry shouts. With a resolve to overhaul him, I jumped on Satan and whirled after the hound.

The black stretched out with such a stride that I was at pains to keep my seat. I dodged the jutting rocks and projecting snags; felt stinging branches in my face and the rush of sweet, dry wind. Under the crumbling walls, over slopes of weathered stone and droppings of shelving rock, round protruding noses of cliff, over and under piñons Satan thundered. He came out on the top of the ridge, at the narrow back I had called a saddle. Here I caught a glimpse of Sounder far below, going down into the ravine from which I had ascended some time before. I called to him, but I might as well have called to the wind.

Weary to the point of exhaustion, I once more turned Satan toward camp. I lay forward on his neck and let him have his will. Far down the ravine I awoke to strange sounds, and soon recognized the cracking of iron-shod hoofs against stone; then voices. Turning an abrupt bend in the sandy wash, I ran into Jones and Wallace.

"Fall in! Line up in the sad procession!" said Jones. "Tige and the pup are faithful. The rest of the dogs are somewhere between the Grand Cañon and the Utah desert."

I related my adventures, and tried to spare Moze and Sounder as much as conscience would permit.

"Hard luck!" commented Jones. "Just as the hounds jumped the cougar—Oh! they bounced him out of the rocks all right—don't you remember, just under that cliff wall where you and Wallace came up to me? Well, just as they jumped him, they ran right into fresh deer tracks. I saw one of the deer. Now that's too much for any hounds, except those trained for lions. I shot at Moze twice, but couldn't turn him. He has to be hurt, they've all got to be hurt to make them understand."

Wallace told of a wild ride somewhere in Jones's wake,

and of sundry knocks and bruises he had sustained, of pieces of corduroy he had left decorating the cedars and of a most humiliating event, where a gaunt and bare piñon snag had penetrated under his belt and lifted him, mad and kicking, off his horse.

"These Western nags will hang you on a limb every chance they get," declared Jones, "and don't you overlook that. Well, there's the cabin. We'd better stay here a few days or a week and break in the dogs and horses, for this day's work was applepie to what we'll get in the Siwash."

I groaned inwardly, and was remorselessly glad to see Wallace fall off his horse and walk on one leg to the cabin. When I got my saddle off Satan, had given him a drink and hobbled him, I crept into the cabin and dropped like a log. I felt as if every bone in my body was broken and my flesh was raw. I got gleeful gratification from Wallace's complaints, and Jones's remark that he had a stitch in his back. So ended the first chase after cougars.

5

Oak Spring

Moze and Don and Sounder straggled into camp next morning, hungry, footsore and scarred; and as they limped in, Jones met them with characteristic speech: "Well, you decided to come in when you got hungry and tired? Never thought of how you fooled me, did you? Now, the first thing you get is a good licking."

He tied them in a little log pen near the cabin and whipped them soundly. And the next few days while Wallace and I rested, he took them out separately and deliberately ran them over coyote and deer trails. Sometimes we heard his stentorian yell as a forerunner to the blast from his old shotgun. Then again we heard the shots unheralded by the yell. Wallace and I waxed warm under the collar over this peculiar method of training dogs, and each of us made dire threats. But in justice to their implacable trainer, the dogs never appeared to be hurt: never a spot of blood flecked their glossy coats, nor did they ever come home limping. Sounder grew wise, and Don gave up but Moze appeared not to change.

"All hands ready to rustle," sang out Frank one morning. "Old Baldy's got to be shod."

This brought us all, except Jones, out of the cabin, to see the object of Frank's anxiety tied to a nearby oak. At first I failed to recognize Old Baldy. Vanished was the slow, sleepy, apathetic manner that had characterized him; his ears lay back on his head; fire flashed from his eyes. When

Frank threw down a kit-bag, which emitted a metallic clanking, Old Baldy sat back on his haunches, planted his forefeet deep in the ground and plainly as a horse could speak, said "No!"

"Sometimes he's bad, and sometimes worse," growled Frank.

"Shore he's plumb bad this mornin'," replied Jim.

Frank got the three of us to hold Baldy's head and pull him up, then he ventured to lift a hind foot over his knee. Old Baldy straightened out his leg and sent Frank sprawling into the dirt. Twice again Frank patiently tried to hold a hind leg, with the same result; and then he lifted a forefoot. Baldy uttered a very intelligible snort, bit through Wallace's glove, yanked Jim off his feet, and scared me so that I let go his forelock. Then he broke the rope which held him to the tree. There was a plunge, a scattering of men, though Jim still valiantly held on to Baldy's head, and a thrashing of scrub piñon, where Baldy reached out vigorously with his hind feet. But for Jim, he would have escaped.

"What's all the row?" called Jones from the cabin. Then from the door, taking in the situation, he yelled: "Hold on, Jim! Pull down on the ornery old cayuse!"

He leaped into action with a lasso in each hand, one whirling round his head. The slender rope straightened with a whiz and whipped round Baldy's legs as he kicked viciously. Jones pulled it tight, then fastened it with nimble fingers to the tree.

"Let go! Let go, Jim!" he yelled, whirling the other lasso. The loop flashed and fell over Baldy's head and tightened round his neck. Jones threw all the weight of his burly form on the lariat, and Baldy crashed to the ground, rolled, tussled, screamed, and then lay on his back, kicking the air with three free legs. "Hold this!" ordered Jones, giving the tight rope to Frank. Whereupon he grabbed my lasso from the saddle, roped Baldy's two forefeet, and pulled him down on his side. This lasso he fastened to a scrub cedar.

"He's chokin'!" said Frank.

"Likely he is," replied Jones shortly. "It'll do him

good." But with his big hands he drew the coil loose and slipped it down over Baldy's nose, where he tightened it again.

"Now, go ahead," he said, taking the rope from Frank.

It had all been done in a twinkling. Baldy lay there groaning and helpless, and when Frank once again took hold of the wicked leg, he was almost passive. When the shoeing operation had been neatly and quickly attended to and Baldy released from his uncomfortable position he struggled to his feet with heavy breaths, shook himself, and looked at his master.

"How'd you like being hog-tied?" queried his conqueror, rubbing Baldy's nose. "Now, after this you'll have some manners."

Old Baldy seemed to understand, for he looked sheepish, and lapsed once more into his listless, lazy unconcern.

"Where's Jim's old cayuse, the pack-horse?" asked our leader.

"Lost. Couldn't find him his morning, an' had a deuce of a time findin' the rest of the bunch. Old Baldy was cute. He hid in a bunch of piñons an' stood quiet so his bell wouldn't ring. I had to trail him."

"Do the horses stray far when they are hobbled?" inquired Wallace.

"If they keep jumpin' all night they can cover some territory. We're now on the edge of the wild horse country, and our nags know this as well as we. They smell the mustangs, an' would break their necks to get away. Satan and the sorrel were ten miles from camp when I found them this mornin'. An' Jim's cayuse went farther, an' we never will get him. He'll wear his hobbles out, then away with the wild horses. Once with them, he'll never be caught again."

On the sixth day of our stay at Oak we had visitors, whom Frank introduced as the Stewart brothers and Lawson, wild-horse wranglers. They were still, dark men, whose facial expression seldom varied; tall and lithe and wiry as the mustangs they rode. The Stewarts were on their way to Kanab, Utah, to arrange for the sale of a drove of horses they had captured and corraled in a narrow cañon back in the Siwash. Lawson said he was at our service, and was promptly hired to look after our horses.

"Any cougar signs back in the breaks?" asked Jones.

"Wal, there's a cougar on every deer trail," replied the elder Stewart, "an' two for every pinto in the breaks. Old Tom himself downed fifteen colts fer us this spring."

"Fifteen colts! That's wholesale murder. Why don't you kill the butcher?"

"We've tried more'n onct. It's a turrible busted up country, them brakes. No man knows it, an' the cougars do. Old Tom ranges all the ridges and brakes, even up on the slopes of Buckskin; but he lives down there in them holes, an' Lord knows, no dog I ever seen could follow him. We tracked him in the snow, an' had dogs after him, but none could stay with him, except two as never cum back. But we've nothin' agin Old Tom like Jeff Clarke, a hoss rustler, who has a string of pintos corraled north of us. Clarke swears he ain't raised a colt in two years."

"We'll put that old cougar up a tree," exclaimed Jones.

"If you kill him we'll make you all a present of a mustang, an' Clarke, he'll give you two each," replied Stewart. "We'd be gettin' rid of him cheap."

"How many wild horses on the mountain now?"

"Hard to tell. Two or three hundred, mebbe. There's almost no ketchin' them, an' they're growin' all the time. We ain't had no luck this spring. The bunch in corral we got last year."

"Seen anythin' of the White Mustang?" inquired Frank. "Ever get a rope near him?"

"No nearer'n we hev fer six years back. He can't be ketched. We seen him an' his band of blacks a few days ago, headin' fer a water-hole down where Nail Cañon runs into Kanab Cañon. He's so cunnin' he'll never water at any of our trap corrals. An' we believe he can go without water fer two weeks, unless mebbe he hes a secret hole we've never trailed him to."

"Would we have any chance to see this White Mustang and his band?" questioned Jones.

"See him? Why, thet'd be easy. Go down Snake Gulch, camp at Singin' Cliffs, go over into Nail Cañon, an' wait.

Then send some one slippin' down to the water-hole at Kanab Cañon, an' when the band cums in to drink—which I reckon will be in a few days now—hev them drive the mustangs up. Only be sure to hev them get ahead of the White Mustang, so he'll hev only one way to cum, fer he sure is knowin'. He never makes a mistake. Mebbe you'll get to see him cum by like a white streak. Why, I've heerd thet mustang's hoofs ring like bells on the rocks a mile away. His hoofs are harder'n any iron shoe as was ever made. But even if you don't get to see him, Snake Gulch is worth seein'."

I learned later from Stewart that the White Mustang was a beautiful stallion of the wildest strain of mustang blue blood. He had roamed the long reaches between the Grand Cañon and Buckskin toward its southern slope for years; he had been the most sought-for horse by all the wranglers, and had become so shy and experienced that nothing but a glimpse was ever obtained of him. A singular fact was that he never attached any of his own species to his band, unless they were coal black. He had been known to fight and kill other stallions, but he kept out of the well-wooded and watered country frequented by other bands, and ranged the brakes of the Siwash as far as he could range. The usual method, indeed the only successful way to capture wild horses, was to build corrals round the water-holes. The wranglers lay out night after night watching. When the mustangs came to drink—which was always after dark—the gates would be closed on them. But the trick had never been tried on the White Mustang, for the simple reason that he never approached one of these traps.

"Boys," said Jones, "seeing we need breaking in, we'll give the White Mustang a little run."

This was most pleasureable news, for the wild horses fascinated me. Besides, I saw from the expression on our leader's face that an uncapturable mustang was an object of interest to him.

Wallace and I had employed the last few warm sunny afternoons in riding up and down the valley below Oak, where there was a fine, level stretch. Here I wore out my soreness of muscle, and gradually overcame my awkwardness in the saddle. Frank's remedy of maple sugar and red pepper had rid me of my cold, and with the return of strength, and the coming of confidence, full, joyous appreciation of wild environment and life made me unspeakably happy. And I noticed that my companions were in like condition of mind, though self-contained where I was exuberant. Wallace galloped his sorrel and watched the crags; Jones talked more kindly to the dogs; Jim baked biscuits indefatigably, and smoked in contented silence; Frank said always: "We'll ooze along easy like, for we've all the time there is." Which sentiment, whether from reiterated suggestion, or increasing confidence in the practical cowboy, or charm of its free import, gradually won us all.

"Boys," said Jones, as we sat round the campfire, "I see you're getting in shape. Well, I've worn off the wire edge myself. And I have the hounds coming fine. They mind me now, but they're mystified. For the life of them they can't understand what I mean. I don't blame them. Wait till, by good luck, we get a cougar in a tree. When Sounder and Don see that, we've lion dogs, boys! we've lion dogs! But Moze is a stubborn brute. In all my years of animal experience, I've never discovered any other way to make animals obey than by instilling fear and respect into their hearts. I've been fond of buffalo, horses and dogs, but sentiment never ruled me. When animals must obey, they must—that's all, and no mawkishness! But I never trusted a buffalo in my life. If I had I wouldn't be here to-night. You all know how many keepers of tame wild animals get killed. I could tell you dozens of tragedies. And I've often thought, since I got back from New York, of that woman I saw with her troop of African lions. I dream about those lions, and see them leaping over her head. What a grand sight that was! But the public is fooled. I read somewhere that she trained those lions by love. I don't believe it. I saw her use a whip and a steel spear. Moreover, I saw many things that escaped most observers—how she entered the cage, how she maneuvered among them, how she kept a compelling gaze on them! It was an admirable, a great piece of work. Maybe she loves those huge yellow brutes, but her life was in danger every moment while she was in that cage, and she knew it. Some day, one of her pets—likely the King of Beasts she pets the most—will rise up and kill her. That is as certain as death."

6

The White Mustang

For thirty miles down Nail Cañon we marked, in every dusty trail and sandy wash, the small, oval, sharply defined tracks of the White Mustang and his band.

The cañon had been well named. It was long, straight and square sided; its bare walls glared steel-gray in the sun, smooth, glistening surfaces that had been polished by wind and water. No weathered heaps of shale, no crumbled piles of stone obstructed its level floor. And, softly toning its drab austerity, here grew the white sage, waving in the breeze, the Indian Paint Brush, with vivid vermilion flower, and patches of fresh, green grass.

"The White King, as we Arizona wild-hoss wranglers calls this mustang, is mighty pertickler about his feed, an' he ranged along here last night, easy like, browsin' on this white sage," said Stewart. Infected by our intense interest in the famous mustang, and ruffled slightly by Jones's manifest surprise and contempt that no one had captured him, Stewart had volunteered to guide us. "Never knowed him to run in this way fer water; fact is, never knowed Nail Cañon hed a fork. It splits down here, but you'd think it was only a crack in the wall. An' thet cunnin' mustang hes been foolin' us fer years about this water-hole."

The fork of Nail Cañon, which Stewart had decided we were in, had been accidentally discovered by Frank, who, in search of our horses one morning, had crossed a ridge, to come suddenly upon the blind, box-like head of the cañon.

Stewart knew the lay of the ridges and run of the cañons as well as any man could know a country where, seemingly, every rod was ridged and bisected, and he was of the opinion that we had stumbled upon one of the White Mustang's secret passages, by which he had so often eluded his pursuers.

Hard riding had been the order of the day, but still we covered ten more miles by sundown. The cañon apparently closed in on us, so camp was made for the night. The horses were staked out, and supper made ready while the shadows were dropping; and when darkness settled thick over us, we lay under our blankets.

Morning disclosed the White Mustang's secret passage. It was a narrow cleft, splitting the cañon wall, rough, uneven, tortuous and choked with fallen rocks—no more than a wonderful crack in solid stone, opening into another cañon. Above us the sky seemed a winding, flowing stream of blue. The walls were so close in places that a horse with pack would have been blocked, and a rider had to pull his legs up over the saddle. On the far side, the passage fell very suddenly for several hundred feet to the floor of the other cañon. No hunter could have seen it, or suspected it from that side.

"This is Grand Cañon country, an' nobody knows what he's goin' to find," was Frank's comment.

"Now we're in Nail Cañon proper," said Stewart, "an' I know my bearin's. I can climb out a mile below an' cut across to Kanab Cañon, an' slip up into Nail Cañon agin, ahead of the mustangs, an' drive 'em up. I can't miss 'em, fer Kanab Cañon is impassable down a little ways. The mustangs will hev to run this way. So all you need do is go below the break, where I climb out, an' wait. You're sure goin' to get a look at the White Mustang. But wait. Don't expect him before noon, an' after thet, any time till he comes. Mebbe it'll be a couple of days, so keep a good watch."

Then taking our man Lawson, with blankets and a knapsack of food, Stewart rode off down the cañon.

We were early on the march. As we proceeded the cañon lost its regularity and smoothness; it became crooked as a rail fence, narrower, higher, rugged and broken. Pinnacled cliffs, cracked and leaning, menaced us from above. Mountains of ruined wall had tumbled into fragments.

It seemed that Jones, after much survey of different corners, angles and points in the cañon floor, chose his position with much greater care than appeared necessary for the ultimate success of our venture—which was simply to see the White Mustang, and if good fortune attended us, to snap some photographs of this wild king of horses. It flashed over me that, with his ruling passion strong within him, our leader was laying some kind of trap for that mustang, was indeed bent on his capture.

Wallace, Frank and Jim were stationed at a point below the break where Stewart had evidently gone up and out. How a horse could have climbed that streaky white slide was a mystery. Jones's instructions to the men were to wait until the mustangs were close upon them, and then yell and shout and show themselves.

He took me to a jutting corner of cliff, which hid us from the others, and here he exercised still more care in scrutinizing the lay of the ground. A wash from ten to fifteen feet wide, and as deep, ran through the cañon in a somewhat meandering course. At the corner which consumed so much of his attention, the dry ditch ran along the cliff wall about fifty feet out; between it and the wall was good level ground; on the other side huge rocks and shale made it hummocky, practically impassable for a horse. It was plain the mustangs, on their way up, would choose the inside of the wash; and here in the middle of the passage, just round the jutting corner, Jones tied our horses to good, strong bushes. His next act was significant. He threw out his lasso and, dragging every crook out of it, carefully recoiled it, and hung it loose over the pommel of his saddle.

"The White Mustang may be yours before dark," he said with the smile that came so seldom. "Now I placed our horses there for two reasons. The mustangs won't see them till they're right on them. Then you'll see a sight and have a chance for a great picture. They will halt; the stallion will prance, whistle and snort for a fight, and then they'll see the saddles and be off. We'll hide across the wash, down a little way, and at the right time we'll shout and yell to drive them up."

By piling sagebrush round a stone, we made a hiding-place. Jones was extremely cautious to arrange the bunches in natural positions. "A Rocky Mountain Big Horn is the only four-footed beast," he said, "that has a better eye than a wild horse. A cougar has an eye, too; he's used to lying high up on the cliffs and looking down for his quarry so as to stalk it at night; but even a cougar has to take second to a mustang when it comes to sight."

The hours passed slowly. The sun baked us; the stones were too hot to touch; flies buzzed behind our ears; tarantulas peeped at us from holes. The afternoon slowly waned.

At dark we returned to where we had left Wallace and the cowboys. Frank had solved the problem of water supply, for he had found a little spring trickling from a cliff, which, by skillful management, produced enough drink for the horses. We had packed our water for camp use.

"You take the first watch to-night," said Jones to me after supper. "The mustangs might try to slip by our fire in the night and we must keep a watch for them. Call Wallace when your time's up. Now, fellows, roll in."

When the pink of dawn was shading white, we were at our posts. A long, hot day—interminably long, deadening to the keenest interest—passed, and still no mustangs came. We slept and watched again, in the grateful cool of night, till the third day broke.

The hours passed; the cool breeze changed to hot; the sun blazed over the cañon wall; the stones scorched; the flies buzzed. I fell asleep in the scant shade of the sage bushes and awoke, stifled and moist. The old plainsman, never weary, leaned with his back against a stone and watched, with narrow gaze, the cañon below. The steely walls hurt my eyes; the sky was like hot copper. Though nearly wild with heat and aching bones and muscles and the long hours of wait—wait—wait, I was ashamed to complain, for there sat the old man, still and silent. I routed out a hairy tarantula from under a stone and teased him into a frenzy with my stick, and tried to get up a fight between him and a scallop-backed horned-toad that blinked wonderingly at me. Then I espied a green lizard on a stone. The beautiful reptile was about a foot in length, bright green, dotted with red, and he had diamonds for eyes. Nearby a purple flower blossomed, delicate and pale, with a bee sucking at its golden heart. I observed then that the lizard had his jewel eyes upon the bee; he slipped to the edge of the stone, flicked out a long, red tongue, and tore the insect from its honeyed perch. Here were beauty, life and death; and I had been weary for something to look at, to think about, to distract me from the wearisome wait!

"Listen!" broke in Jones's sharp voice. His neck was stretched, his eyes were closed, his ear was turned to the wind.

With thrilling, reawakened eagerness, I strained my hearing. I caught a faint sound, then lost it.

"Put your ear to the ground," said Jones.

I followed his advice, and detected the rhythmic beat of galloping horses.

"The mustangs are coming, sure as you're born!" exclaimed Jones.

"There! See the cloud of dust!" cried he a minute later.

In the first bent of the cañon below, a splintered ruin of rock now lay under a rolling cloud of dust. A white flash appeared, a line of bobbing black objects, and more dust; then with a sharp pounding of hoofs, into clear vision shot a dense black band of mustangs, and well in front swung the White King.

"Look! Look! I never saw the beat of that—never in my born days!" cried Jones. "How they move! yet that white fellow isn't half-stretched out. Get your picture before they pass. You'll never see the beat of that."

With long manes and tails flying, the mustangs came on apace and passed us in a trampling roar, the white stallion in the front. Suddenly a shrill, whistling blast, unlike any sound I had ever heard, made the cañon fairly ring. The white stallion plunged back, and his band closed in behind him. He had seen our saddle horses. Then trembling, whinnying, and with arched neck and high-poised head, bespeaking his mettle, he advanced a few paces, and again whistled his shrill note of defiance. Pure creamy white he was, and built like a racer. He pranced, struck his hoofs hard and cavorted; then, taking sudden fright, he wheeled.

It was then, when the mustangs were pivoting, with the white in the lead, that Jones jumped upon the stone, fired his pistol and roared with all his strength. Taking his cue, I did likewise. The band huddled back again, uncertain and frightened, then broke up the cañon.

Jones jumped the ditch with surprising agility, and I followed close at his heels. When we reached our plunging horses, he shouted: "Mount, and hold this passage. Keep close in by that big stone at the turn so they can't run you down, or stampede you. If they head your way, scare them back."

Satan quivered, and when I mounted, reared and plunged. I had to hold him in hard, for he was eager to run. At the cliff wall I was at some pains to check him. He kept champing his bit and stamping his feet.

From my post I could see the mustangs flying before a cloud of dust. Jones was turning in his horse behind a large rock in the middle of the cañon, where he evidently intended to hide. Presently successive yells and shots from our comrades blended in a roar which the narrow box-cañon augmented and echoed from wall to wall. High the White Mustang reared, and above the roar whistled his snort of furious terror. His band wheeled with him and charged back, their hoofs ringing like hammers on iron.

The crafty old buffalo-hunter had hemmed the mustangs in a circle and had left himself free in the center. It was a wily trick, born of his quick mind and experienced eye.

The stallion, closely crowded by his followers, moved swiftly. I saw that he must pass near the stone. Thundering, crashing, the horses came on. Away beyond them I saw Frank and Wallace. Then Jones yelled to me: "Open up! open up!"

I turned Satan into the middle of the narrow passage,

screaming at the top of my voice and discharging my revolver rapidly.

But the wild horses thundered on. Jones saw that they would not now be balked, and he spurred his bay directly in their path. The big horse, courageous as his intrepid master, dove forward.

Then followed confusion for me. The pound of hoofs, the snorts, a screaming neigh that was frightful, the mad stampede of the mustangs with a whirling cloud of dust, bewildered and frightened me so that I lost sight of Jones. Danger threatened and passed me almost before I was aware of it. Out of the dust a mass of tossing manes, foam-flecked black horses, wild eyes and lifting hoofs rushed at me. Satan, with a presence of mind that shamed mine, leaped back and hugged the wall. My eyes were blinded by dust; the smell of dust choked me. I felt a strong rush of wind and a mustang grazed my stirrup. Then they had passed, on the wings of the dust-laden breeze.

But not all, for I saw that Jones had, in some inexplicable manner, cut the White Mustang and two of his blacks out of the band. He had turned them back again and was pursuing them. The bay he rode had never before appeared to much advantage, and now, with his long, lean, powerful body in splendid action, imbued with the relentless will of his rider, what a picture he presented! How he did run! With all that, the White Mustang made him look dingy and slow. Nevertheless, it was a critical time in the wild career of that king of horses. He had been penned in a space two hundred by five hundred yards, half of which was separated from him by a wide ditch, a yawning chasm that he had refused; and behind him, always keeping on the inside, wheeled the yelling hunter, who savagely spurred his bay and whirled a deadly lasso. He had been cut off and surrounded; the very nature of the rocks and trails of the cañon threatened to end his freedom or his life. Certain it was he preferred to end the latter, for he risked death from the rocks as he went over them in long leaps.

Jones could have roped either of the two blacks, but he hardly noticed them. Covered with dust and splotches of foam, they took their advantage, turned on the circle toward the passage way and galloped by me out of sight. Again Wallace, Frank and Jim let out strings of yells and volleys. The chase was narrowing down. Trapped, the White Mustang King had no chance. What a grand spirit he showed! Frenzied as I was with excitement, the thought occurred to me that this was an unfair battle, that I ought to stand aside and let him pass. But the blood and lust of primitive instinct held me fast. Jones, keeping back, met his every turn. Yet always with lithe and beautiful stride the stallion kept out of reach of the whirling lariat.

"Close in!" yelled Jones, and his voice, powerful with a note of triumph, bespoke the knell of the king's freedom.

The trap closed in. Back and forth at the upper end the White Mustang worked; then rendered desperate by the closing in, he circled round nearer to me. Fire shone in his wild eyes. The wily Jones was not to be outwitted; he kept in the middle, always on the move, and he yelled to me to open up. I lost my voice again, and fired my last shot. Then the White Mustang burst into a dash of daring, despairing speed. It was his last magnificent effort. Straight for the wash at the upper end he pointed his racy, spirited head, and his white legs stretched far apart, twinkled and stretched again. Jones galloped to cut him off, and the yells he emitted were demoniacal. It was a long, straight race for the mustang, a short curve for the bay.

That the white stallion gained was as sure as his resolve to elude capture, and he never swerved a foot from his course. Jones might have headed him, but manifestly he wanted to ride with him, as well as to meet him, so in case the lasso went true, a terrible shock might be averted.

Up went Jones's arm as the space shortened, and the lasso ringed his head. Out it shot, lengthened like a yellow, striking snake, and fell just short of the flying white tail.

The White Mustang, fulfilling his purpose in a last heroic display of power, sailed into the air, up and up, and over the wide wash like a white streak. Free! the dust rolled in a cloud from under his hoofs, and he vanished.

Jones's superb horse, crashing down on his haunches, just escaped sliding into the hole.

I awoke to the realization that Satan had carried me, in

pursuit of the thrilling chase, all the way across the circle without my knowing it.

Jones calmly wiped the sweat from his face, calmly coiled his lasso, and calmly remarked:

"In trying to capture wild animals a man must never be too sure. Now what I thought my strong point was my weak point—the wash. I made sure no horse could ever jump that hole."

7

Snake Gulch

Not far from the scene of our adventures with the White Streak, as we facetiously and appreciatively named the mustang, a deep, flat cave indented the cañon wall. By reason of its sandy floor and close proximity to Frank's trickling spring, we decided to camp in it. About dark, Lawson and Stewart straggled in on spent horses, and found awaiting them a bright fire, a hot supper and cheery comrades.

"Did yu fellars git to see him?" was the tall ranger's first question.

"Did we get to see him?" echoed five lusty voices as one. "We did!"

It was after Frank, in his plain, blunt speech, had told of our experience, that the long Arizonian gazed fixedly at Jones.

"Did yu acktully tech the hair of thet mustang with a rope?"

In all his days Jones never had a greater compliment. By way of reply, he moved his big hand to a button of his coat, and, fumbling over it, unwound a string of long, white hairs, then said: "I pulled these out of his tail with my lasso; it missed his left hind hoof about six inches."

There were six of the hairs, pure, glistening white, and over three feet long. Stewart examined them in expressive silence, then passed them along; and when they reached me, they stayed.

The cave, lighted up by a blazing fire, appeared to me a forbidding, uncanny place. Small, peculiar round holes, and dark cracks, suggestive of hidden vermin, gave me a creepy feeling; and although not over-sensitive on the subject of crawling, creeping things, I voiced my disgust.

"Say, I don't like the idea of sleeping in this hole. I'll bet it's full of spiders, snakes and centipedes and other poisonous things."

Whatever there was in my inoffensive declaration to rouse the usually slumbering humor of the Arizonians, and the thinly veiled ridicule of Colonel Jones, and a mixture of both in my once loyal California friend, I am not prepared to state. Maybe it was the dry, sweet, cool air of Nail Cañon; maybe my suggestion awoke ticklish associations that worked themselves off thus; maybe it was the first instance of my committing myself to a breach of camp etiquette. Be that as it may, my innocently expressed sentiment gave rise to bewildering dissertations on entomology, and most remarkable and startling tales from first-hand experience.

"Like as not," began Frank in matter-of-fact tone. "Them's tarantuler holes all right. An' scorpions, centipedes an' rattlers always rustle with tarantulers. But we never mind them—not us fellers! We're used to sleepin' with them. Why, I often wake up in the night to see a big tarantuler on my chest, an' see him wink. Ain't thet so, Jim?"

"Shore as hell," drawled faithful, slow Jim.

"Reminds me how fatal the bite of a centipede is," took up Colonel Jones, complacently. "Once I was sitting in camp with a hunter, who suddenly hissed out: 'Jones, for God's sake don't budge! There's a centipede on your arm!' He pulled his Colt, and shot the blamed centipede off as clean as a whistle. But the bullet hit a steer in the leg; and would you believe it, the bullet carried so much poison that in less than two hours the steer died of blood poisoning. Centipedes are so poisonous they leave a blue trail on flesh just by crawling over it. Look there!"

He bared his arm, and there on the brown-corded

flesh was a blue trail of something, that was certain. It might have been made by a centipede.

"This is a likely place for them," put in Wallace, emitting a volume of smoke and gazing round the cave walls with the eye of a connoisseur. "My archæological pursuits have given me great experience with centipedes, as you may imagine, considering how many old tombs, caves and cliff-dwellings I have explored. This Algonkian rock is about the right stratum for centipedes to dig in. They dig somewhat after the manner of the fluviatile long-tailed decapod crustaceans, of the genera *Thoracostraca*, the common crawfish, you know. From that, of course, you can imagine, if a centipede can bite rock, what a biter he is."

I began to grow weak, and did not wonder to see Jim's long pipe fall from his lips. Frank looked queer around the gills, so to speak, but the gaunt Steward never batted an eye.

"I camped here two years ago," he said, "an' the cave was alive with rock-rats, mice, snakes, horned-toads, lizards an' a big Gila monster, besides bugs, scorpions, rattlers, an' as fer tarantulers an' centipedes—say! I couldn't sleep fer the noise they made fightin'."

"I seen the same," concluded Lawson, as nonchalant as a wild-horse wrangler well could be. "An' as fer me, now I allus lays perfickly still when the centipedes an' tarantulers begin to drop from their holes in the roof, same as them holes up there. An' when they light on me, I never move, nor even breathe fer about five minutes. Then they take a notion I'm dead an' crawl off. But sure, if I'd breathed I'd been a goner!"

All of this was playfully intended for the extinction of an unoffending and impressionable tenderfoot.

With an admiring glance at my tormentors, I rolled out my sleeping-bag and crawled into it, vowing I would remain there even if devil-fish, armed with pikes, invaded our cave.

Late in the night I awoke. The bottom of the cañon and the outer floor of our cave lay bathed in white, clear moonlight. A dense, gloomy black shadow veiled the opposite cañon wall. High up the pinnacles and turrets pointed toward a resplendent moon. It was a weird, wonderful scene of beauty entrancing, of breathless, dreaming silence that seemed not of life. Then a hoot-owl lamented dismally, his call fitting the scene and the dead stillness; the echoes resounded from cliff to cliff, strangely mocking and hollow, at last reverberating low and mournful in the distance.

How long I lay there enraptured with the beauty of night and mystery of shade, thrilling at the lonesome lament of the owl, I have no means to tell; but I was awakened from my trance by the touch of something crawling over me. Promptly I raised my head. The cave was as light as day. There, sitting sociably on my sleeping-bag was a great black tarantula, as large as my hand.

For one still moment, notwithstanding my contempt for Lawson's advice, I certainly acted upon it to the letter. If ever I was quiet, and if ever I was cold, the time was then. My companions snored in blissful ignorance of my plight. Slight rustling sounds attracted my wary gaze from the old black sentinel on my knee. I saw other black spiders running to and fro on the silver, sandy floor. A giant, as large as a soft-shell crab, seemed to be meditating an assault upon Jones's ear. Another, grizzled and shiny with age or moonbeams—I could not tell which—pushed long, tentative feelers into Wallace's cap. I saw black spots darting over the roof. It was not a dream; the cave was alive with tarantulas!

Not improbably my strong impression that the spider on my knee deliberately winked at me was the result of memory, enlivening imagination. But it sufficed to bring to mind, in one rapid, consoling flash, the irrevocable law of destiny—that the deeds of the wicked return unto them again.

I slipped back into my sleeping bag, with a keen consciousness of its nature, and carefully pulled the flap in place, which almost hermetically sealed me up.

"Hey ! Jones! Wallace! Frank! Jim!" I yelled, from the depths of my safe refuge.

Wondering cries gave me glad assurance that they had awakened from their dreams.

"The cave's alive with tarantulas!" I cried, trying to hide my unholy glee.

"I'll be durned if it ain't!" ejaculated Frank.

"Shore it beats hell!" added Jim, with a shake of his blanket.

"Look out, Jones, there's one on your pillow!" shouted Wallace.

Whack! A sharp blow proclaimed the opening of hostilities.

Memory stamped indelibly every word of that incident; but innate delicacy prevents the repetition of all save the old warrior's concluding remarks: "! ! !——place I was ever in! Tarantulas by the million—centipedes, scorpions, bats! Rattlesnakes, too, I'll swear. Look out, Wallace! there, under your blanket!"

From the shuffling sounds which wafted sweetly into my bed, I gathered that my long friend from California must have gone through motions creditable to a contortionist. An ensuing explosion from Jones proclaimed to the listening world that Wallace had thrown a tarantula upon him. Further fearful language suggested the thought that Colonel Jones had passed on the inquisitive spider to Frank. The reception accorded the unfortunate tarantula, no doubt scared out of its wits, began with a wild yell from Frank and ended in pandemonium.

While the confusion kept up, with whacks and blows and threshing about, with language such as never before had disgraced a group of old campers, I choked with rapture, and reveled in the sweetness of revenge.

When quiet reigned once more in the black and white cañon, only one sleeper lay on the moon-silvered sand of the cave.

At dawn, when I opened sleepy eyes, Frank, Jim, Stewart and Lawson had departed, as pre-arranged, with the outfit, leaving the horses belonging to us and rations for the day. Wallace and I wanted to climb the divide at the break, and go home by way of Snake Gulch, and the Colonel acquiesced with the remark that his sixty-three years had taught him there was much to see in the world. Coming to undertake it, we found the climb—except for a slide of weathered rock—no great task, and we accomplished it in half an hour, with breath to spare and no mishap to horses.

But descending into Snake Gulch, which was only a mile across the sparsely cedared ridge, proved to be tedious labor. By virtue of Satan's patience and skill, I forged ahead; which advantage, however, meant more risk for me because of the stones set in motion above. They rolled and bumped and cut into me, and I sustained many a bruise trying to protect the sinewy slender legs of my horse. The descent ended without serious mishap.

Snake Gulch had a character and sublimity which cast Nail Cañon into the obscurity of forgetfulness. The great contrast lay in the diversity of structure. The rock was bright red, with parapet of yellow, that leaned, heaved, bulged outward. These emblazoned cliff walls, two thousand feet high, were cracked from turret to base; they bowled out at such an angle that we were afraid to ride under them. Mountains of yellow rock hung balanced, ready to tumble down at the first angry breath of the gods. We rode among carved stones, pillars, obelisks and sculptured ruined walls of a fallen Babylon. Slides reaching all the way across and far up the cañon wall obstructed our passage. On every stone silent green lizards sunned themselves, gliding swiftly as we came near to their marble homes.

We came into a region of wind-worn caves, of all sizes and shapes, high and low on the cliffs; but strange to say, only on the north side of the cañon they appeared with dark mouths open and uninviting. One, vast and deep, though far off, menaced us as might the cave of a tawny-maned king of beasts; yet it impelled, fascinated and drew us on.

"It's a long, hard climb," said Wallace to the Colonel, as we dismounted.

"Boys, I'm with you," came the reply. And he was with us all the way, as we clambered over the immense blocks and threaded a passage between them and pulled weary legs up, one after the other. So steep lay the jumble of cliff fragments that we lost sight of the cave long before we got near it. Suddenly we rounded a stone, to halt and gasp at the thing looming before us.

The dark portal of death or hell might have yawned there. A gloomy hole, large enough to admit a church, had been hollowed in the cliff by ages of nature's chiseling.

"Vast sepulcher of Time's past, give up thy dead!" cried Wallace, solemnly.

"Oh! dark Stygian cave forlorn!" quoted I, as feelingly as my friend.

Jones hauled us down from the clouds.

"Now, I wonder what kind of a prehistoric animal holed in here," said he.

Forever the one absorbing interest! If he realized the sublimity of this place, he did not show it.

The floor of the cave ascended from the very threshold. Stony ridges circled from wall to wall. We climbed till we were two hundred feet from the opening, yet we were not half-way to the dome. Our horses, browsing in the sage far below, looked like ants. So steep did the ascent become that we desisted; for if one of us had slipped on the smooth incline, the result would have been terrible. Our voices rang clear and hollow from the walls. We were so high that the sky was blotted out by the overhanging square, cornice-like top of the door; and the light was weird, dim, shadowy, opaque. It was a gray tomb.

"Waa-hoo!" yelled Jones with all the power of his wide, leather lungs.

Thousands of devilish voices rushed at us, seemingly on puffs of wind. Mocking, deep echoes bellowed from the ebon shades at the back of the cave, and the walls, taking them up, hurled them on again in fiendish concatenation.

We did not again break the silence of that tomb, where the spirits of ages lay in dusty shrouds; and we crawled down as if we had invaded a sanctuary and invoked the wrath of the gods.

We all proposed names: Montezuma's Amphitheater being the only rival of Jones's selection, Echo Cave, which we finally chose.

Mounting our horses again, we made twenty miles of Snake Gulch by noon, when we rested for lunch. All the way up we had played the boy's game of spying for sights, with the honors about even. It was a question if Snake Gulch ever before had such a raking over. Despite its name, however, we discovered no snakes.

From the sandy niche of a cliff where we lunched Wallace espied a tomb, and heralded his discovery with a victorious whoop. Digging in old ruins roused in him much the same spirit that digging in old books roused in me. Before we reached him, he had a big bowie-knife buried deep in the red, sandy floor of the tomb.

This one-time sealed house of the dead had been constructed of small stones, held together by a cement, the nature of which, Wallace explained, had never become clear to civilization. It was red in color and hard as flint, harder than the rocks it glued together. The tomb was half-round in shape, and its floor was a projecting shelf of cliff rock. Wallace unearthed bits of pottery, bone and finely braided rope, all of which, to our great disappointment, crumbled to dust in our fingers. In the case of the rope, Wallace assured us, this was a sign of remarkable antiquity.

In the next mile we traversed, we found dozens of these old cells, all demolished except a few feet of the walls, all despoiled of their one-time possessions. Wallace thought these depredations were due to Indians of our own time. Suddenly we came upon Jones, standing under a cliff, with his neck craned to a desperate angle.

"Now, what's that?" demanded he, pointing upward.

High on the cliff wall appeared a small, round protuberance. It was of the unmistakably red color of the other tombs; and Wallace, more excited than he had been in the cougar chase, said it was a sepulcher, and he believed it had never been opened.

From an elevated point of rock, as high up as I could well climb, I decided both questions with my glass. The tomb resembled nothing so much as a mud-wasp's nest, high on a barn wall. The fact that it had never been broken open quite carried Wallace away with enthusiasm.

"This is no mean discovery, let me tell you that," he declared. "I am familiar with the Aztec, Toltec and Pueblo ruins, and here I find no similarity. Besides, we are out of their latitude. An ancient race of people—very ancient indeed—lived in this cañon. How long ago, it is impossible to tell."

"They must have been birds," said the practical Jones. "Now, how'd that tomb ever get there? Look at it, will you?"

As near as we could ascertain, it was three hundred feet from the ground below, five hundred from the rim wall above, and could not possibly have been approached from the top. Moreover, the cliff wall was as smooth as a wall of human make.

"There's another one," called out Jones.

"Yes, and I see another; no doubt there are many of them," replied Wallace. "In my mind, only one thing possible accounts for their position. You observe they appear to be about level with each other. Well, once the cañon floor ran along that line, and in the ages gone by it has lowered, washed away by the rains."

This conception staggered us, but it was the only one conceivable. No doubt we all thought at the same time of the little rainfall in that arid section of Arizona.

"How many years?" queried Jones.

"Years! What are years?" said Wallace. "Thousands of years, ages have passed since the race who built these tombs lived."

Some persuasion was necessary to drag our scientific friend from the spot, where obviously helpless to do anything else, he stood and gazed longingly at the isolated tombs. The cañon widened as we proceeded; and hundreds of points that invited inspection, such as overhanging shelves of rock, dark fissures, caverns and ruins had to be passed by, for lack of time.

Still, a more interesting and important discovery was to come, and the pleasure and honor of it fell to me. My eyes were sharp and peculiarly farsighted—the Indian sight, Jones assured me; and I kept them searching the walls in such places as my companions overlooked. Presently, under a large, bulging bluff, I saw a dark spot, which took the shape of a figure. This figure, I recollected, had been presented to my sight more than once, and now it stopped me. The hard climb up the slippery stones was fatiguing, but I did not hesitate, for I was determined to know. Once upon the ledge, I let out a yell that quickly set my companions in my direction. The figure I had seen was a dark, red devil, a painted image, rude, unspeakably wild, crudely executed, but painted by the hand of man. The whole surface of the cliff wall bore figures of all shapes— men, animals, birds and strange devices, some in red paint, mostly in yellow. Some showed the wear of time· others were clear and sharp.

Wallace puffed up to me, but he had wind enough left for another whoop. Jones puffed up also, and seeing the first thing a rude sketch of what might have been a deer or a buffalo, he commented thus: "Darn me if I ever saw an animal like that! Boys, this is a find, sure as you're born. Because not even the Piutes ever spoke of these figures. I doubt if they know they're here. And the cowboys and wranglers, what few ever get by here in a hundred years, never saw these things. Beats anything I ever saw on the Mackenzie, or anywhere else."

The meaning of some devices was as mystical as that of others was clear. Two blood-red figures of men, the larger dragging the smaller by the hair, while he waved aloft a blood-red hatchet or club, left little to conjecture. Here was the old battle of men, as old as life. Another group, two figures of which resembled the foregoing in form and action, battling over a prostrate form rudely feminine in outline, attested to an age when men was as susceptible as they are in modern times, but more forceful and original. An odd yellow Indian waved aloft a red hand, which striking picture suggested the idea that he was an ancient Macbeth, listening to the knocking at the gate. There was a character representing a great chief, before whom many figures lay prostrate, evidently slain or subjugated. Large red paintings, in the shape of bats, occupied prominent positions, and must have represented gods or devils. Armies of marching men told of that blight of nations old and young—war. These, and birds unnamable, and beasts unclassable, with dots and marks and hieroglyphics, recorded the history of a bygone people. Symbols they were of an era that had gone into the dim past, leaving only these marks, forever unintelligible; yet while they stood, century after century, ineffaceable, reminders of the glory, the mystery, the sadness of life.

"How could paint of any kind last so long?" asked Jones, shaking his head doubtfully.

"That is the unsolvable mystery," returned Wallace. "But the records are there. I am absolutely sure the paintings are at least a thousand years old. I have never seen any tombs or paintings similar to them. Snake Gulch is a find, and I shall some day study its wonders."

Sundown caught us within sight of Oak Spring, and we soon trotted into camp to the welcoming chorus of the hounds. Frank and the others had reached the cabin some hours before. Supper was steaming on the hot coals with a delicious fragrance.

Then came the pleasantest time of the day, after a long chase or jaunt—the silent moments, watching the glowing embers of the fire; the speaking moments when a red-blooded story rang clear and true; the twilight moments, when the wood-smoke smelled sweet.

Jones seemed unusually thoughtful. I had learned that this preoccupation in him meant the stirring of old associations, and I waited silently. By and by Lawson snored mildly in a corner; Jim and Frank crawled into their blankets, and all was still. Wallace smoked his Indian pipe and hunted in firelit dreams.

"Boys," said our leader finally, "somehow the echoes dying away in that cave reminded me of the mourn of the big white wolves in the Barren Lands."

Wallace puffed huge clouds of white smoke, and I waited, knowing that I was to hear at last the story of the Colonel's great adventure in the Northland.

8

Naza! Naza! Naza!

It was a waiting day at Fort Chippewayan. The lonesome, far-northern Hudson's Bay Trading Post seldom saw such life. Tepees dotted the banks of the Slave River and lines of blanketed Indians paraded its shores. Near the boat landing a group of chiefs, grotesque in semi-barbaric, semi-civilized splendor, but black-browed, austere-eyed, stood in savage dignity with folded arms and high-held heads. Lounging on the grassy bank were white men, traders, trappers and officials of the post.

All eyes were on the distant curve of the river where, as it lost itself in a fine-fringed bend of dark green, white-glinting waves danced and fluttered. A June sky lay blue in the majestic stream; ragged, spear-topped, dense green trees massed down to the water; beyond rose bold, bald-knobbed hills, in remote purple relief.

A long Indian arm stretched south. The waiting eyes discerned a black speck on the green, and watched it grow. A flatboat, with a man standing to the oars, bore down swiftly.

Not a red hand, nor a white one, offered to help the voyager in the difficult landing. The oblong, clumsy, heavily laden boat surged with the current and passed the dock despite the boatman's efforts. He swung his craft in below upon a bar and roped it fast to a tree. The Indians crowded above him on the bank. The boatman raised his powerful form erect, lifted a bronzed face which seemed set in craggy hardness, and cast from narrow eyes a keen, cool glance on those above. The silvery gleam in his fair hair told of years.

Silence, impressive as it was ominous, broke only to the rattle of camping paraphernalia, which the voyager threw to a level, grassy bench on the bank. Evidently this unwelcome visitor had journeyed from afar, and his boat, sunk deep into the water with its load of barrels, boxes and bags, indicated that the journey had only begun. Significant, too, were a couple of long Winchester rifles shining on a tarpaulin.

The cold-faced crowd stirred and parted to permit the passage of a tall, thin, gray personage of official bearing, in a faded military coat.

"Are you the musk-ox hunter?" he asked, in tones that contained no welcome.

The boatman greeted this peremptory interlocutor with a cool laugh—a strange laugh, in which the muscles of his face appeared not to play.

"Yes, I am the man," he said.

"The chiefs of the Chippewayan and Great Slave tribes have been apprised of your coming. They have held council and are here to speak with you."

At a motion from the commandant, the line of chieftains piled down to the level bench and formed a half-circle before the voyager. To a man who had stood before grim Sitting Bull and noble Black Thunder of the Sioux, and faced the falcon-eyed Geronimo, and glanced over the sights of a rifle at gorgeous-feathered, wild, free Comanches, this semi-circle of savages—lords of the north— was a sorry comparison. Bedaubed and betrinketed, slouchy, and slovenly, these low-statured chiefs belied in appearance their scorn-bright eyes and lofty mien. They made a sad group.

One who spoke in unintelligible language, rolled out a haughty, sonorous voice over the listening multitude. When he had finished, a half-breed interpreter, in the dress of a white man, spoke at a signal from the commandant.

"He says listen to the great orator of the Chippewayan.

He has summoned all the chiefs of the tribes south of Great Slave Lake. He has held council. The cunning of the pale-face, who comes to take the musk-oxen, is well known. Let the pale-face hunter return to his own hunting-grounds; let him turn his face from the north. Never will the chiefs permit the white man to take musk-oxen alive from their country. The Ageter, the Musk-ox, is their god. He gives them food and fur. He will never come back if he is taken away, and the reindeer will follow him. The chiefs and their people would starve. They command the pale-face hunter to go back. They cry Naza! Naza! Naza!"

"Say, for a thousand miles I've heard that word Naza!" returned the hunter, with mingled curiosity and disgust. "At Edmonton Indian runners started ahead of me, and every village I struck the redskins would crowd round me and an old chief would harangue at me, and motion me back, and point north with Naza! Naza! Naza! What does it mean?"

"No white man knows; no Indian will tell," answered the interpreter. "The traders think it means the Great Slave, the North Star, the North Spirit, the North Wind, the North Lights and Ageter, the musk-ox god."

"Well, say to the chiefs to tell Ageter I have been four moons on the way after some of his little Ageters, and I'm going to keep on after them."

"Hunter, you are most unwise," broke in the commandant, in his officious voice. "The Indians will never permit you to take a musk-ox alive from the north. They worship him, pray to him. It is a wonder you have not been stopped."

"Who'll stop me?"

"The Indians. They will kill you if you do not turn back."

"Faugh! to tell an American plainsman that!" The hunter paused a steady moment, with his eyelids narrowing over slits of blue fire. "There is no law to keep me out, nothing but Indian superstition and the greed of the Hudson's Bay people. And I am an old fox, not to be fooled by pretty baits. For years the officers of this fur-trading company have tried to keep out explorers. Even Sir John

Franklin, an Englishman, could not buy food of them. The policy of the company is to side with the Indians, to keep out traders and trappers. Why? So they can keep on cheating the poor savages out of clothing and food by trading a few trinkets and blankets, a little tobacco and rum for millions of dollars worth of furs. Have I failed to hire man after man, Indian after Indian, not to know why I cannot get a helper? Have I, a plainsman, come a thousand miles alone to be scared by you, or a lot of craven Indians? Have I been dreaming of musk-oxen for forty years, to slink south now, when I begin to feel the north? Not I."

Deliberately every chief, with the sound of a hissing snake, spat in the hunter's face. He stood immovable while they perpetrated the outrage, then calmly wiped his cheeks, and in his strange, cool voice, addressed the interpreter.

"Tell them thus they show their true qualities, to insult in council. Tell them they are not chiefs, but dogs. Tell them they are not even squaws, only poor, miserable starved dogs. Tell them I turn my back on them. Tell them the paleface has fought real chiefs, fierce, bold, like eagles, and he turns his back on dogs. Tell them he is the one who could teach them to raise the musk-oxen and the reindeer, and to keep out the cold and the wolf. But they are blinded. Tell them the hunter goes north."

Through the council of chiefs ran a low mutter, as of gathering thunder.

True to his word, the hunter turned his back on them. As he brushed by, his eye caught a gaunt savage slipping from the boat. At the hunter's stern call, the Indian leaped ashore, and started to run. He had stolen a parcel, and would have succeeded in eluding its owner but for an unforeseen obstacle, as striking as it was unexpected.

A white man of colossal stature had stepped in the thief's passage, and laid two great hands on him. Instantly the parcel flew from the Indian, and he spun in the air to fall into the river with a sounding splash. Yells signaled the surprise and alarm caused by this unexpected incident. The Indian frantically swam to the shore. Whereupon the champion of the stranger in a strange land lifted a bag, which gave forth a musical clink of steel, and throwing it with the camp articles on the grassy bench, he extended a huge, friendly hand.

"My name is Rea," he said, in deep, cavernous tones.

"Mine is Jones," replied the hunter, and right quickly did he grip the proffered hand. He saw in Rea a giant, of whom he was but a stunted shadow. Six and one-half feet Rea stood, with yard-wide shoulders, a hulk of bone and brawn. His ponderous, shaggy head rested on a bull neck. His broad face, with its low forehead, its close-shut mastiff under jaw, its big, opaque eyes, pale and cruel as those of a jaguar, marked him a man of terrible brute force.

"Free-trader!" called the commandant. "Better think twice before you join fortunes with the musk-ox hunter."

"To hell with you an' your rantin', dog-eared redskins!" cried Rea. "I've run agin a man of my own kind, a man of my own country, an' I'm goin' with him."

With this he thrust aside some encroaching, gaping Indians so unconcernedly and ungently that they sprawled upon the grass.

Slowly the crowd mounted and once more lined the bank.

Jones realized that by some late-turning stroke of fortune, he had fallen in with one of the few free-traders of the province. These free-traders, from the very nature of their calling—which was to defy the fur company, and to trap and trade on their own account—were a hardy and intrepid class of men. Rea's worth to Jones exceeded that of a dozen ordinary men. He knew the ways of the north, the language of the tribes, the habits of animals, the handling of dogs, the uses of food and fuel. Moreover, it soon appeared that he was a carpenter and blacksmith.

"There's my kit," he said, dumping the contents of his bag. It consisted of a bunch of steel traps, some tools, a broken ax, a box of miscellaneous things such as trappers used, and a few articles of flannel. "Thievin' redskins," he added, in explanation of his poverty. "Not much of an outfit. But I'm the man for you. Besides, I had a pal onct who knew you on the plains, called you 'Buff' Jones. Old Jim Bent he was."

"I recollect Jim," said Jones. "He went down in Custer's last charge. So you were Jim's pal. That'd be a recommendation if you needed one. But the way you chucked the Indian overboard got me."

Rea soon manifested himself as a man of few words and much action. With the planks Jones had on board he heightened the stern and bow of the boat to keep out the beating waves in the rapids; he fashioned a steering-gear and a less awkward set of oars, and shifted the cargo so as to make more room in the craft.

"Buff, we're in for a storm. Set up a tarpaulin an' make a fire. We'll pretend to camp to-night. These Indians won't dream we'd try to run the river after dark, and we'll slip by under cover."

The sun glazed over; clouds moved up from the north; a cold wind swept the tips of the spruces, and rain commenced to drive in gusts. By the time it was dark not an Indian showed himself. They were housed from the storm. Lights twinkled in the tepees and the big log cabins of the trading company. Jones scouted round till pitchy black night, when a freezing, pouring blast sent him back to the protection of the tarpaulin. When he got there he found that Rea had taken it down and awaited him. "Off!" said the free-trader; and with no more noise than a drifting feather the boat swung into the current and glided down till the twinkling fires no longer accentuated the darkness.

By night the river, in common with all swift rivers, had a sullen voice, and murmured its hurry, its restraint, its menace, its meaning. The two boatmen, one at the steering gear, one at the oars, faced the pelting rain and watched the dim, dark line of trees. The craft slid noiselessly onward into the gloom.

And into Jones's ears, above the storm, poured another sound, a steady, muffled rumble, like the roll of giant chariot wheels. It had come to be a familiar roar to him, and the only thing which, in his long life of hazard, had ever sent the cold, prickling, tight shudder over his warm skin. Many times on the Athabasca that rumble had presaged the dangerous and dreaded rapids.

"Hell Bend Rapids!" shouted Rea. "Bad water, but no rocks."

The rumble expanded to a roar, the roar to a boom that charged the air with heaviness, with a dreamy burr. The whole indistinct world appeared to be moving to the lash of wind, to the sound of rain, to the roar of the river. The boat shot down and sailed aloft, met shock on shock, breasted leaping dim white waves, and in a hollow, unearthly blend of watery sounds, rode on and on, buffeted, tossed, pitched into a black chaos that yet gleamed with obscure shrouds of light. Then the convulsive stream shrieked out a last defiance, changed its course abruptly to slow down and drown the sound of rapids in muffling distance. Once more the craft swept on smoothly, to the drive of the wind and the rush of the rain.

By midnight the storm cleared. Murky clouds split to show shining, blue-white stars and a fitful moon, that silvered the crests of the spruces and sometimes hid like a gleaming, black-threaded pearl behind the dark branches.

Jones, a plainsman all his days, wonderingly watched the moon-blanched water. He saw it shade and darken under shadowy walls of granite, where it swelled with hollow song and gurgle. He heard again the far-off rumble, faint on the night wind. High cliff banks appeared, walled out the mellow light, and the river suddenly narrowed. Yawning holes, whirlpools of a second, opened with a gurgling suck and raced with the boat.

On the craft flew. Far ahead, a long, declining plane of jumping frosted waves played dark and white with the moonbeams. The Slave plunged to his freedom, down his riven, stone-spiked bed, knowing no patient eddy, and white-wreathed his dark, shiny rocks in spume and spray.

9

The Land of the Musk-Ox

A far cry it was from bright June at Port Chippewayan to dim October on Great Slave Lake.

Two long, laborious months Rea and Jones threaded the crooked shores of the great inland sea, to halt at the extreme northern end, where a plunging outlet formed the source of a river. Here they found a stone chimney and fireplace standing among the darkened, decayed ruins of a cabin.

"We mustn't lose no time," said Rea. "I feel the winter in the wind. An' see how dark the days are gettin' on us."

"I'm for hunting musk-oxen," replied Jones.

"Man, we're facin' the northern night; we're in the land of the midnight sun. Soon we'll be shut in for seven months. A cabin we want, an' wood, an' meat."

A forest of stunted spruce trees edged on the lake, and soon its dreary solitudes rang to the strokes of axes. The trees were small and uniform in size. Black stumps protruded, here and there, from the ground, showing work of the steel in time gone by. Jones observed that the living trees were no larger in diameter than the stumps, and questioned Rea in regard to the difference in age.

"Cut twenty-five, mebbe fifty years ago," said the trapper.

"But the living trees are no bigger."

"Trees an' things don't grow fast in the northland."

They erected a fifteen-foot cabin round the stone

chimney, roofed it with poles and branches of spruce, and a layer of sand. In digging near the fireplace Jones unearthed a rusty file and the head of a whisky keg, upon which was a sunken word in unintelligible letters.

"We've found the place," said Rea. "Franklin built a cabin here in 1819. An' in 1833 Captain Back wintered here when he was in search of Captain Ross of the vessel *Fury*. It was those explorin' parties thet cut the trees. I seen Indian sign out there, made last winter, I reckon; but Indians never cut down no trees."

The hunters completed the cabin, piled cords of firewood outside, stowed away the kegs of dried fish and fruits, the sacks of flour, boxes of crackers, canned meats and vegetables, sugar, salt, coffee, tobacco—all of the cargo; then took the boat apart and carried it up the bank, which labor took them less than a week.

Jones found sleeping in the cabin, despite the fire, uncomfortably cold, because of the wide chinks between the logs. It was hardly better than sleeping under the swaying spruces. When he essayed to stop up the cracks—a task by no means easy, considering the lack of material—Rea laughed his short "Ho! Ho!" and stopped him with the word, "Wait." Every morning the green ice extended farther out into the lake; the sun paled dim and dimmer; the nights grew colder. On October 8th the thermometer registered several degrees below zero; it fell a little more next night and continued to fall.

"Ho! Ho!" cried Rea. "She's struck the toboggan, an' presently she'll commence to slide. Come on, Buff, we've work to do."

He caught up a bucket, made for their hole in the ice, rebroke a six-inch layer, the freeze of a few hours, and filling his bucket, returned to the cabin. Jones had no inkling of the trapper's intention, and wonderingly he soused his bucket full of water and followed.

By the time he had reached the cabin, a matter of some thirty or forty good paces, the water no longer splashed from his pail, for a thin film of ice prevented. Rea stood fifteen feet from the cabin, his back to the wind, and threw the water. Some of it froze in the air, most of it froze on the logs. The simple plan of the trapper to incase the cabin with ice was easily divined. All day the men worked, ceasing only when the cabin resembled a glistening mound. It had not a sharp corner nor a crevice. Inside it was warm and snug, and as light as when the chinks were open.

A slight moderation of the weather brought the snow. Such snow! A blinding white flutter of great flakes, as large as feathers! All day they rustled softly; all night they swirled, sweeping, seeping, brushing against the cabin. "Ho! Ho!" roared Rea. "'Tis good; let her snow, an' the reindeer will migrate. We'll have fresh meat." The sun shone again, but not brightly. A nipping wind cut down out of the frigid north and crusted the snow. The third night following the storm, when the hunters lay snug under their blankets, a commotion outside aroused them.

"Indians," said Rea, "come north for reindeer."

Half the night, shouting and yelling, barking of dogs, hauling of sleds and cracking of dried-skin tepees murdered sleep for those in the cabin. In the morning the level plain and edge of the forest held an Indian village. Caribou hides, strung on forked poles, constituted tent-like habitations with no distinguishable doors. Fires smoked in the holes in the snow. Not till late in the day did any life manifest itself round the tepees, and then a group of children, poorly clad in ragged pieces of blankets and skins, gaped at Jones. He saw their pinched, brown faces, staring, hungry eyes, naked legs and throats, and noted particularly their dwarfish size. When he spoke they fled precipitously a little way, then turned. He called again, and all ran except one small lad. Jones went into the cabin and came out with a handful of sugar in square lumps.

"Yellow Knife Indians," said Rea. "A starved tribe! We're in for it."

Jones made motions to the lad, but he remained still, as if transfixed, and his black eyes stared wonderingly.

"Molar nasu (white man good)," said Rea.

The lad came out of his trance and looked back at his companions, who edged nearer. Jones ate a lump of sugar, then handed one to the little Indian. He took it gingerly, put it into his mouth and immediately jumped up and down.

"Hoppieshampoolie! Hoppieshampoolie!" he shouted to his brothers and sisters. They came on the run.

"Think he means sweet salt," interpreted Rea. "Of course these beggars never tasted sugar."

The band of youngsters trooped round Jones, and after tasting the white lumps, shrieked in such delight that the braves and squaws shuffled out of the tepees.

In all his days Jones had never seen such miserable Indians. Dirty blankets hid all their person, except straggling black hair, hungry, wolfish eyes and moccasined feet. They crowded into the path before the cabin door and mumbled and stared and waited. No dignity, no brightness, no suggestion of friendliness marked this peculiar attitude.

"Starved!" exclaimed Rea. "They've come to the lake to invoke the Great Spirit to send the reindeer. Buff, whatever you do, don't feed them. If you do, we'll have them on our hands all winter. It's cruel, but, man, we're in the north!"

Notwithstanding the practical trapper's admonition Jones could not resist the pleading of the children. He could not stand by and see them starve. After ascertaining there was absolutely nothing to eat in the tepees, he invited the little ones into the cabin, and made a great pot of soup, into which he dropped compressed biscuits. The savage children were like wildcats. Jones had to call in Rea to assist him in keeping the famished little aborigines from tearing each other to pieces. When finally they were all fed, they had to be driven out of the cabin.

"That's new to me," said Jones. "Poor little beggars!"

Rea doubtfully shook his shaggy head.

Next day Jones traded with the Yellow Knives. He had a goodly supply of baubles, besides blankets, gloves and boxes of canned goods, which he had brought for such trading. He secured a dozen of the large-boned, white and black Indian dogs—huskies, Rea called them—two long sleds with harness and several pairs of snowshoes. This trade made Jones rub his hands in satisfaction, for during all the long journey north he had failed to barter for such cardinal necessities to the success of his venture.

"Better have doled out the grub to them in rations," grumbled Rea.

Twenty-four hours sufficed to show Jones the wisdom of the trapper's words, for in just that time the crazed, ignorant savages had glutted the generous store of food, which should have lasted them for weeks. The next day they were begging at the cabin door. Rea cursed and threatened them with his fists, but they returned again and again.

Days passed. All the time, in light and dark, the Indians filled the air with dismal chant and doleful incantations to the Great Spirit, and the tum! tum! tum! tum! of tomtoms, a specific feature of their wild prayer for food.

But the white monotony of the rolling land and level lake remained unbroken. The reindeer did not come. The days became shorter, dimmer, darker. The mercury kept on the slide.

Forty degrees below zero did not trouble the Indians. They stamped till they dropped, and sang till their voices vanished, and beat the tomtoms everlastingly. Jones fed the children once each day, against the trapper's advice.

One day, while Rea was absent, a dozen braves succeeded in forcing an entrance, and clamored so fiercely, and threatened so desperately, that Jones was on the point of giving them food when the door opened to admit Rea.

With a glance he saw the situation. He dropped the bucket he carried, threw the door wide open and commenced action. Because of his great bulk he seemed slow, but every blow of his sledge-hammer fist knocked a brave against the wall, or through the door into the snow. When he could reach two savages at once, by way of diversion, he swung their heads together with a crack. They dropped like dead things. Then he handled them as if they were sacks of corn, pitching them out into the snow. In two minutes the cabin was clear. He banged the door and slipped the bar in place.

"Buff, I'm goin' to get mad at these thievin' redskins some day," he said gruffly. The expanse of his chest heaved slightly, like the slow swell of a calm ocean, but there was no other indication of unusual exertion.

Jones laughed, and again gave thanks for the comradeship of this strange man.

Shortly afterward, he went out for wood, and as usual scanned the expanse of the lake. The sun shone mistier and wanner, and frost feathers floated in the air. Sky and sun and plain and lake—all were gray. Jones fancied he saw a distant moving mass of darker shade than the gray background. He called the trapper.

"Caribou," said Rea instantly. "The vanguard of the migration. Hear the Indians! Hear their cry: 'Aton! Aton!' they mean reindeer. The idiots have scared the herd with their infernal racket, an' no meat will they get. The caribou will keep to the ice, an' man or Indian can't stalk them there."

For a few moments his companion surveyed the lake and shore with a plainsman's eye, then dashed within, to reappear with a Winchester in each hand. Through the crowd of bewailing, bemoaning Indians he sped, to the low, dying bank. The hard crust of snow upheld him. The gray cloud was a thousand yards out upon the lake and moving southeast. If the caribou did not swerve from this course they would pass close to a projecting point of land, a half-mile up the lake. So, keeping a wary eye upon them, the hunter ran swiftly. He had not hunted antelope and buffalo on the plains all his life without learning how to approach moving game. As long as the caribou were in action, they could not tell whether he moved or was motionless. In order to tell if an object was inanimate or not, they must stop to see, of which fact the keen hunter took advantage. Suddenly he saw the gray mass slow down and bunch up. He stopped running, to stand like a stump. When the reindeer moved again, he moved, and when they slackened again, he stopped and became motionless. As they kept to their course, he worked gradually closer and closer. Soon he distinguished gray, bobbing heads. When the leader showed signs of halting in his slow trot the hunter again became a statue. He saw they were easy to deceive; and, daringly confident of success, he encroached

on the ice and closed up the gap till not more than two
hundred yards separated him from the gray, bobbing,
antlered mass.

Jones dropped on one knee. A moment only his eyes
lingered admiringly on the wild and beautiful spectacle;
then he swept one of the rifles to a level. Old habit made
the little beaded sight cover first the stately leader. Bang!
The gray monarch leaped straight forward, forehoofs up,
antlered head back, to fall dead with a crash. Then for a few
moments the Winchester spat a deadly stream of fire, and
when emptied was thrown down for the other gun, which in
the steady, sure hands of the hunter belched death to the
caribou.

The herd rushed on, leaving the white surface of the
lake gray with a struggling, kicking, bellowing heap. When
Jones reached the caribou he saw several trying to rise on
crippled legs. With his knife he killed these, not without
some hazard to himself. Most of the fallen ones were
already dead, and the others soon lay still. Beautiful gray
creatures they were, almost white, with wide-reaching,
symmetrical horns.

A medley of yells arose from the shore, and Rea
appeared running with two sleds, with the whole tribe of
Yellow Knives pouring out of the forest behind him.

"Buff, you're jest what old Jim said you was," thundered Rea, as he surveyed the gray pile. "Here's winter
meat, an' I'd not have given a biscuit for all the meat I
thought you'd get."

"Thirty shots in less than thirty seconds," said Jones,
"an' I'll bet every ball I sent touched hair. How many
reindeer?"

"Twenty! twenty! Buff, or I've forgot how to count. I
guess mebbe you can't handle them shootin' arms. Ho! here
comes the howlin' redskins."

Rea whipped out a bowie knife and began disembow-
eling the reindeer. He had not proceeded far in his task
when the crazed savages were around him. Every one
carried a basket or receptacle, which he swung aloft, and
they sang, prayed, rejoiced on their knees. Jones turned
away from the sickening scenes that convinced him these

savages were little better than cannibals. Rea cursed them, and tumbled them over, and threatened them with the big bowie. An altercation ensued, heated on his side, frenzied on theirs. Thinking some treachery might befall his comrade, Jones ran into the thick of the group.

"Share with them, Rea, share with them."

Whereupon the giant hauled out ten smoking carcasses. Bursting into a babel of savage glee and tumbling over one another, the Indians pulled the caribou to the shore.

"Thievin' fools!" growled Rea, wiping the sweat from his brow. "Said they'd prevailed on the Great Spirit to send the reindeer. Why, they'd never smelled warm meat but for you. Now, Buff, they'll gorge every hair, hide an' hoof of their share in less than a week. Thet's the last we do for the damned cannibals. Didn't you see them eatin' of the raw innards?—faugh! I'm calculatin' we'll see no more reindeer. It's late for the migration. The big herd has driven southward. But we're lucky, thanks to your prairie trainin'. Come on now with the sleds, or we'll have a pack of wolves to fight."

By loading three reindeer on each sled, the hunters were not long in transporting them to the cabin. "Buff, there ain't much doubt about them keepin' nice and cool," said Rea. "They'll freeze, an' we can skin them when we want."

That night the starved wolf dogs gorged themselves till they could not rise from the snow. Likewise the Yellow Knives feasted. How long the ten reindeer might have served the wasteful tribe, Rea and Jones never found out. The next day two Indians arrived with dog-trains, and their advent was hailed with another feast, and a pow-wow that lasted into the night.

"Guess we're goin' to get rid of our blasted hungry neighbors," said Rea, coming in next morning with the water pail, "an' I'll be durned, Buff, if I don't believe them crazy heathen have been told about you. Them Indians was messengers. Grab your gun, an' let's walk over and see."

The Yellow Knives were breaking camp, and the hunters were at once conscious of the difference in their bearing. Rea addressed several braves, but got no reply. He laid his broad hand on the old wrinkled chief, who repulsed him, and turned his back. With a growl, the trapper spun the Indian round, and spoke as many words of the language as he knew. He got a cold response, which ended in the ragged old chief starting up, stretching a long, dark arm northward, and with eyes fixed in fanatical subjection, shouting: "Naza! Naza! Naza!"

"Heathen!" Rea shook his gun in the faces of the messengers. "It'll go bad with you to come Nazain' any longer on our trail. Come, Buff, clear out before I get mad."

When they were once more in the cabin, Rea told Jones that the messengers had been sent to warn the Yellow Knives not to aid the white hunters in any way. That night the dogs were kept inside, and the men took turns in watching. Morning showed a broad trail southward. And with the going of the Yellow Knives the mercury dropped to fifty, and the long, twilight winter night fell.

So with this agreeable riddance and plenty of meat and fuel to cheer them, the hunters sat down in their snug cabin to wait many months for daylight.

Those few intervals when the wind did not blow were the only times Rea and Jones got out of doors. To the plainsman, new to the north, the dim gray world about him was of exceeding interest. Out of the twilight shone a wan, round, lusterless ring that Rea said was the sun. The silence and desolation were heart-numbing.

"Where are the wolves?" asked Jones of Rea.

"Wolves can't live on snow. They're farther south after caribou, or farther north after musk-ox."

In those few still intervals Jones remained out as long as he dared, with the mercury sinking to sixty degrees. He turned from the wonder of the unreal, remote sun, to the marvel in the north—Aurora borealis—ever-present, ever-changing, ever-beautiful! and he gazed in rapt attention.

"Polar lights," said Rea, as if he were speaking of biscuits. "You'll freeze. It's gettin' cold."

Cold it became, to the matter of seventy degrees. Frost covered the walls of the cabin and the roof, except just over the fire. The reindeer were harder than iron. A knife or an ax or a steel-trap burned as if it had been heated in fire, and stuck to the hand. The hunters experienced trouble in breathing; the air hurt their lungs.

The months dragged. Rea grew more silent day by day, and as he sat before the fire his wide shoulders sagged lower and lower. Jones, unaccustomed to the waiting, the restraint, the barrier of the north, worked on guns, sleds, harness, till he felt he would go mad. Then to save his mind he constructed a windmill of caribou hides and pondered over it trying to invent, to put into practical use an idea he had once conceived.

Hour after hour he lay under his blankets unable to sleep, and listened to the north wind. Sometimes Rea mumbled in his slumbers; once his giant form started up, and he muttered a woman's name. Shadows from the fire flickered on the walls, visionary, spectral shadows, cold and gray, fitting the north. At such times he longed with all the power of his soul to be among those scenes far southward, which he called home. For days Rea never spoke a word, only gazed into the fire, ate and slept. Jones, drifting far from his real self, feared the strange mood of the trapper and sought to break it, but without avail. More and more he reproached himself, and singularly on the one fact that, as he did not smoke himself, he had brought only a small store of tobacco. Rea, inordinate and inveterate smoker, had puffed away all the weed in clouds of white, then had relapsed into gloom.

10

Success and Failure

A t last the marvel in the north dimmed, the obscure gray shade lifted, the hope in the south brightened, and the mercury climbed—reluctantly, with a tyrant's hate to relinquish power.

Spring weather at twenty-five below zero! On April 12th a small band of Indians made their appearance. Of the Dog tribe were they, an offcast of the Great Slaves, according to Rea, and as motley, staring and starved as the Yellow Knives. But they were friendly, which presupposed ignorance of the white hunters, and Rea persuaded the strongest brave to accompany them as guide northward after musk-oxen.

On April 16th, having given the Indians several caribou carcasses, and assuring them that the cabin was protected by white spirits, Rea and Jones, each with sled and train of dogs, started out after their guide, who was similarly equipped, over the glistening snow toward the north. They made sixty miles the first day, and pitched their Indian tepee on the shores of Artillery Lake. Traveling northeast, they covered its white waste of one hundred miles in two days. Then a day due north, over rolling, monotonously snowy plain, devoid of rock, tree or shrub, brought them into a country of the strangest, queerest little spruce trees, very slender, and none of them over fifteen feet in height. A primeval forest of saplings.

"Ditchen Nechila!" said the guide.

"Land of Sticks Little," translated Rea.

An occasional reindeer was seen and numerous foxes and hares trotted off into the woods, evincing more curiosity than fear. All were silver white, even the reindeer, at a distance, taking the hue of the north. Once a beautiful creature, unblemished as the snow it trod, ran up a ridge and stood watching the hunters. It resembled a monster dog, only it was inexpressibly more wild looking.

"Ho! Ho! there you are!" cried Rea, reaching for his Winchester. "Polar wolf! Them's the white devils we'll have hell with."

As if the wolf understood, he lifted his white, sharp head and uttered a bark or howl that was like nothing so much as a haunting, unearthly mourn. The animal then merged into the white, as if he were really a spirit of the world whence his cry seemed to come.

In this ancient forest of youthful appearing trees, the hunters cut firewood to the full carrying capacity of the sleds. For five days the Indian guide drove his dogs over the smooth crust, and on the sixth day, about noon, halting in a hollow, he pointed to tracks in the snow and called out: "Ageter! Ageter! Ageter!"

The hunters saw sharply defined hoof-marks, not unlike the tracks of reindeer, except that they were longer. The tepee was set up on the spot and the dogs unharnessed.

The Indian led the way with the dogs, and Rea and Jones followed, slipping over the hard crust without sinking in and traveling swiftly. Soon the guide, pointing, again let out the cry: "Ageter!" at the same moment loosing the dogs.

Some few hundred yards down the hollow, a number of large black animals, not unlike the shaggy, humpy buffalo, lumbered over the snow. Jones echoed Rea's yell, and broke into a run, easily distancing the puffing giant.

The musk-oxen squared round to the dogs, and were soon surrounded by the yelping pack. Jones came up to find six old bulls uttering grunts of rage and shaking ram-like horns at their tormentors. Notwithstanding that for Jones this was the cumulation of years of desire, the crowning moment, the climax and fruition of long-harbored dreams, he halted before the tame and helpless beasts, with joy not unmixed with pain.

"It will be murder!" he exclaimed. "It's like shooting down sheep."

Rea came crashing up behind him and yelled: "Get busy. We need fresh meat, an' I want the skins."

The bulls succumbed to well-directed shots, and the Indian and Rea hurried back to camp with the dogs to fetch the sleds, while Jones examined with warm interest the animals he had wanted to see all his life. He found the largest bull approached within a third of the size of a buffalo. He was of a brownish-black color and very like a large, woolly ram. His head was broad, with sharp, small ears; the horns had wide and flattened bases and lay flat on the head, to run down back of the eyes, then curve forward to a sharp point. Like the bison, the musk-ox had short, heavy limbs, covered with very long hair, and small, hard hoofs with hairy tufts inside the curve of bone, which probably served as pads or checks to hold the hoof firm on ice. His legs seemed out of proportion to his body.

Two musk-oxen were loaded on a sled and hauled to camp in one trip. Skinning them was but short work for such expert hands. All the choice cuts of meat were saved. No time was lost in broiling a steak, which they found sweet and juicy, with a flavor of musk that was disagreeable.

"Now, Rea, for the calves," exclaimed Jones, "and then we're homeward bound."

"I hate to tell this redskin," replied Rea. "He'll be like the others. But it ain't likely he'd desert us here. He's far from his base, with nothin' but thet old musket." Rea then commanded the attention of the brave, and began to mangle the Great Slave and Yellow Knife languages. Of this mixture Jones knew but few words. "Ageter nechila," which Rea kept repeating, he knew, however, meant "musk-oxen little."

The guide stared, suddenly appeared to get Rea's meaning, then vigorously shook his head and gazed at Jones in fear and horror. Following this came an action as singular as inexplicable. Slowly rising, he faced the north, lifted his hand, and remained statuesque in his immobility. Then he began deliberately packing his blankets and traps on his sled, which had not been unhitched from the train of dogs.

"Jackoway ditchen hula," he said, and pointed south.

"Jackoway ditchen hula," echoed Rea. "The damned Indian says 'wife sticks none.' He's goin' to quit us. What do you think of thet? His wife's out of wood. Jackoway out of wood, and' here we are two days from the Arctic Ocean! Jones, the damned heathen don't go back!"

The trapper coolly cocked his rifle. The savage, who plainly saw and understood the action, never flinched. He turned his breast to Rea, and there was nothing in his demeanor to suggest his relation to a craven tribe.

"Good heavens, Rea, don't kill him!" exclaimed Jones, knocking up the leveled rifle.

"Why not, I'd like to know!" demanded Rea, as if he were considering the fate of a threatening beast. "I reckon it'd be a bad thing for us to let him go."

"Let him go," said Jones. "We are here on the ground. We have dogs and meat. We'll get our calves and reach the lake as soon as he does, and we might get there before."

"Mebbe we will," growled Rea.

No vacillation attended the Indian's mood. From a friendly guide, he had suddenly been transformed into a dark, sullen savage. He refused the musk-ox meat offered by Jones, and he pointed south and looked at the white hunters as if he asked them to go with him. Both men shook their heads in answer. The savage struck his breast a sounding blow and with his index finger pointed at the white of the north, he shouted dramatically: "Naza! Naza! Naza!"

He then leaped upon his sled, lashed his dogs into a run, and without looking back disappeared over a ridge.

The musk-ox hunters sat long silent. Finally Rea shook his shaggy locks and roared. "Ho! Ho! Jackoway out of wood! Jackoway out of wood! Jackoway out of wood!"

On the day following the desertion, Jones found tracks to the north of the camp, making a broad trail in which were numerous little imprints that sent him flying back to get Rea and the dogs. Musk-oxen in great numbers had passed in the night, and Jones and Rea had not trailed the herd a mile before they had it in sight. When the dogs burst into full cry, the musk-oxen climbed a high knoll and squared about to give battle.

"Calves! Calves! Calves!" cried Jones.

"Hold back! Hold back! Thet's a big herd, an' they'll show fight."

As good fortune would have it, the herd split up into several sections, and one part, hard pressed by the dogs, ran down the knoll, to be cornered under the lee of a bank. The hunters, seeing this small number, hurried upon them to find three cows and five badly frightened little calves backed against the bank of snow, with small red eyes fastened on the barking, snapping dogs.

To a man of Jones's experience and skill, the capturing of the calves was a ridiculously easy piece of work. The cows tossed their heads, watched the dogs, and forgot their young. The first cast of the lasso settled over the neck of a little fellow. Jones hauled him out over the slippery snow and laughed as he bound the hairy legs. In less time than he had taken to capture one buffalo calf, with half the effort, he had all the little musk-oxen bound fast. Then he signaled this feat by pealing out an Indian yell of victory.

"Buff, we've got 'em," cried Rea; "an' now for the hell of it—gettin' 'em home. I'll fetch the sleds. You might as well down thet best cow for me. I can use another skin."

Of all Jones's prizes of captured wild beasts—which numbered nearly every species common to western North America—he took greatest pride in the little musk-oxen. In truth, so great had been his passion to capture some of these rare and inaccessible mammals, that he considered the day's work the fulfillment of his life's purpose. He was happy. Never had he been so delighted as when, the very evening of their captivity, the musk-oxen, evincing no particular fear of him, began to dig with sharp hoofs into the snow for moss. And they found moss, and ate it, which solved Jones's greatest problem. He had hardly dared to think how to feed them, and here they were picking sustenance out of the frozen snow.

"Rea, will you look at that! Rea, will you look at that!" he kept repeating. "See, they're hunting feed."

And the giant, with his rare smile, watched him play with the calves. They were about two and a half feet high, and resembled long-haired sheep. The ears and horns were undiscernible, and their color considerably lighter than that of the matured beasts.

"No sense of fear of man," said the life-student of animals. "But they shrink from the dogs."

In packing for the journey south, the captives were strapped on the sleds. This circumstance necessitated a sacrifice of meat and wood, which brought grave, doubtful shakes of Rea's great head.

Days of hastening over the icy snow, with short hours for sleep and rest, passed before the hunters awoke to the consciousness that they were lost. The meat they had packed had gone to feed themselves and the dogs. Only a few sticks of wood were left.

"Better kill a calf, an' cook meat while we've got a little wood left," suggested Rea.

"Kill one of my calves? I'd starve first!" cried Jones.

The hungry giant said no more.

They headed southwest. All about them glared the grim monotony of the arctics. No rock or bush or tree made a welcome mark upon the hoary plain. Wonderland of frost, white marble desert, infinitude of gleaming silences!

Snow began to fall, making the dogs flounder, obliterating the sun by which they traveled. They camped to wait for clearing weather. Biscuits soaked in tea made their meal. At dawn Jones crawled out of the tepee. The snow had ceased. But where were the dogs? He yelled in alarm. Then little mounds of white, scattered here and there, became animated, heaved, rocked and rose to fall to pieces, exposing the dogs. Blankets of snow had been their covering.

Rea had ceased his "Jackoway out of wood," for a reiterated question: "Where are the wolves?"

"Lost," replied Jones in hollow humor.

Near the close of that day, in which they had resumed travel, from the crest of a ridge they descried a long, low, undulating dark line. It proved to be the forest of "little sticks," where, with grateful assurance of fire and of soon finding their old trail, they made camp.

"We've four biscuits left, an' enough tea for one drink each," said Rea. "I calculate we're two hundred miles from Great Slave Lake. Where are the wolves?"

At that moment the night wind wafted through the forest a long, haunting mourn. The calves shifted uneasily; the dogs raised sharp noses to sniff the air, and Rea, settling back against a tree, cried out: "Ho! Ho!" Again the savage sound, a keen wailing note with the hunger of the northland in it, broke the cold silence. "You'll see a pack of real wolves in a minute," said Rea. Soon a swift pattering of feet down a forest slope brought him to his feet with a curse to reach a brawny hand for his rifle. White streaks crossed the black of the tree trunks; then indistinct forms, the color of snow, swept up, spread out and streaked to and fro. Jones thought the great, gaunt, pure white beasts the spectral wolves of Rea's fancy, for they were silent, and silent wolves must belong to dreams only.

"Ho! Ho!" yelled Rea. "There's green-fire eyes for you, Buff. Hell itself ain't nothin' to these white devils. Get the calves in the tepee, an' stand ready to loose the dogs, for we've got to fight."

Raising his rifle he opened fire upon the white foe. A struggling, rustling sound followed the shots. But whether it was the threshing about of wolves dying in agony, or the fighting of the fortunate ones over those shot, could not be ascertained in the confusion.

Following his example Jones also fired rapidly on the other side of the tepee. The same inarticulate, silently rustling wrestle succeeded this volley.

"Wait!" cried Rea. "Be sparin' of cartridges."

The dogs strained at their chains and bravely bayed the wolves. The hunters heaped logs and brush on the fire, which, blazing up, sent a bright light far into the woods. On the outer edge of that circle moved the white, restless, gliding forms.

"They're more afraid of fire than of us," said Jones.

So it proved. When the fire burned and crackled they kept well in the background. The hunters had a long respite from serious anxiety, during which time they collected all the available wood at hand. But at midnight, when this had been mostly consumed, the wolves grew bold again.

"Have you any shots left for the 45–90, besides what's in the magazine?" asked Rea.

"Yes, a good handful."

"Well, get busy."

With careful aim Jones emptied the magazine into the gray, gliding, groping mass. The same rustling, shuffling, almost silent strife ensued.

"Rea, there's something uncanny about those brutes. A silent pack of wolves!"

"Ho! Ho!" rolled the giant's answer through the woods.

For the present the attack appeared to have been effectually checked. The hunters, sparingly adding a little of their fast diminishing pile of fuel to the fire, decided to lie down for much needed rest, but not for sleep. How long they lay there, cramped by the calves, listening for stealthy steps, neither could tell; it might have been moments and might have been hours. All at once came a rapid rush of pattering feet, succeeded by a chorus of angry barks, then a terrible commingling of savage snarls, growls, snaps and barks.

"Out!" yelled Rea. "They're on the dogs!"

Jones pushed his cocked rifle ahead of him and straightened up outside the tepee. A wolf, large as a steer and white as the gleaming snow, sprang at him. As he discharged his rifle, right against the breast of the beast, he saw its dripping jaws, its wicked green eyes, the spurts of fire and felt its hot breath. It fell at his feet and writhed in the death struggle. Slender bodies of black and white, whirling and tussling together, sent out fiendish uproar. Rea threw a blazing stick of wood among them, which sizzled as it met the furry coats, and brandishing another he ran into the thick of the fight. Unable to stand the proximity of fire, the wolves bolted and loped off into the woods.

"What a huge brute!" exclaimed Jones, dragging the one he had shot into the light. It was a superb animal, thin, supple, strong, with a coat of frosty fur, very long and fine.

Rea began at once to skin it, remarking that he hoped to find other pelts in the morning.

Through the wolves remained in the vicinity of camp, none ventured near. The dogs moaned and whined; their restlessness increased as dawn approached, and when the gray light came, Jones found that some of them had been badly lacerated by the fangs of the wolves. Rea hunted for dead wolves and found not so much as a piece of white fur.

Soon the hunters were speeding southward. Other than a disposition to fight among themselves, the dogs showed no evil effects of the attack. They were lashed to their best speed, for Rea said the white rangers of the north would never quit their trail. All day the men listened for the wild, lonesome, haunting mourn. But it came not.

A wonderful halo of white and gold, that Rea called a sun-dog, hung in the sky all afternoon, and dazzlingly bright over the dazzling world of snow, circled and glowed a mocking sun, brother of the desert mirage, beautiful illusion, smiling cold out of the polar blue.

The first pale evening star twinkled in the east when the hunters made camp on the shore of Artillery Lake. At dusk the clear, silent air opened to the sound of a long, haunting mourn.

"Ho! Ho!" called Rea. His hoarse, deep voice rang defiance to the foe.

While he built a fire before the tepee, Jones strode up and down, suddenly to whip out his knife and make for the tame little musk-oxen, now digging in the snow. Then he wheeled abruptly and held out the blade to Rea.

"What for?" demanded the giant.

"We've got to eat," said Jones. "And I can't kill one of them. I can't, so you do it."

"Kill one of our calves?" roared Rea. "Not till hell freezes over! I ain't commenced to get hungry. Besides, the wolves are going to eat us, calves and all."

Nothing more was said. They ate their last biscuit. Jones packed the calves away in the tepee, and turned to the dogs. All day they had worried him; something was amiss with them, and even as he went among them a fierce fight broke out. Jones saw it was unusual, for the attacked dogs showed craven fear, and the attacking ones a howling, savage intensity that surprised him. Then one of the vicious brutes rolled his eyes, frothed at the mouth, shuddered and leaped in his harness, vented a hoarse howl and fell back shaking and retching.

"My God! Rea!" cried Jones in horror. "Come here! Look! That dog is dying of rabies! Hydrophobia! The white wolves have hydrophobia!"

"If you ain't right!" exclaimed Rea. "I seen a dog die of thet onct, an' he acted like this. An' thet one ain't all. Look, Buff! look at them green eyes! Didn't I say the white wolves was hell? We'll have to kill every dog we've got."

Jones shot the dog, and soon afterward three more that manifested signs of the disease. It was an awful situation. To kill all the dogs meant simply to sacrifice his life and Rea's; it meant abandoning hope of ever reaching the cabin. Then to risk being bitten by one of the poisoned, maddened brutes, to risk the most horrible of agonizing deaths—that was even worse.

"Rea, we've one chance," cried Jones, with pale face. "Can you hold the dogs, one by one, while I muzzle them?"

"Ho! Ho!" replied the giant. Placing his bowie knife between his teeth, with gloved hands he seized and dragged one of the dogs to the campfire. The animal whined and protested, but showed no ill spirit. Jones muzzled his jaws tightly with strong cords. Another and another were tied up, then one which tried to snap at Jones was nearly crushed by the giant's grip. The last, a surly brute, broke out into mad ravings the moment he felt the touch of Jones's hands, and writhing, frothing, he snapped Jones's sleeve. Rea jerked him loose and flung him in the air with one arm, while with the other he swung the bowie. They hauled the dead dogs out on the snow, and returning to the fire sat down to await the cry they expected.

Presently, as darkness fastened down tight, it came—the same cry, wild, haunting, mourning. But for hours it was not repeated.

"Better rest some," said Rea; "I'll call you if they come."

Jones dropped to sleep as he touched his blankets.

Morning dawned for him, to find the great, dark, shadowy figure of the giant nodding over the fire.

"How's this? Why didn't you call me?" demanded Jones.

"The wolves only fought a little over the dead dogs."

On the instant Jones saw a wolf skulking up the bank. Throwing up his rifle, which he had carried out of the tepee, he took a snap-shot at the beast. It ran off on three legs, to go out of sight over the bank. Jones scrambled up the steep, slippery place, and upon arriving at the ridge, which took several moments of hard work, he looked everywhere for the wolf. In a moment he saw the animal, standing still some hundred or more paces down a hollow. With the quick report of Jones's second shot, the wolf fell and rolled over. The hunter ran to the spot to find the wolf was dead. Taking hold of a front paw, he dragged the animal over the snow to camp. Rea began to skin the animal, when suddenly he exclaimed:

"This fellow's hind foot is gone!"

"That's strange. I saw it hanging by the skin as the wolf ran up the bank. I'll look for it."

By the bloody trail on the snow he returned to the place where the wolf had fallen, and thence back to the spot where its leg had been broken by the bullet. He discovered no sign of the foot.

"Didn't find it, did you?" said Rea.

"No, and it appears odd to me. The snow is so hard the foot could not have sunk."

"Well, the wolf ate his foot, thet's what," returned Rea. "Look at them teeth marks!"

"Is it possible?" Jones stared at the leg Rea held up.

"Yes, it is. These wolves are crazy at times. You've seen thet. An' the smell of blood, an' nothin' else, mind you, in my opinion, made him eat his own foot. We'll cut him open."

Impossible as the thing seemed to Jones—and he could not but believe further evidence of his own eyes—it was even stranger to drive a train of mad dogs. Yet that was what Rea and he did, and lashed them, beat them to cover many miles in the long day's journey. Rabies had broken out in several dogs so alarmingly that Jones had to kill them at the end of the run. And hardly had the sound of the shots died when faint and far away, but clear as a bell, bayed on the wind the same haunting mourn of a trailing wolf.

"Ho! Ho! where are the wolves?" cried Rea.

A waiting, watching, sleepless night followed. Again the hunters faced the south. Hour after hour, riding, running, walking, they urged the poor, jaded, poisoned dogs. At dark they reached the head of Artillery Lake. Rea placed the tepee between two huge stones. Then the hungry hunters, tired, grim, silent, desperate, awaited the familiar cry.

It came on the cold wind, the same haunting mourn, dreadful in its significance.

Absence of fire inspirited the wary wolves. Out of the pale gloom gaunt white forms emerged, agile and stealthy, slipping on velvet-padded feet, closer, closer, closer. The dogs wailed in terror.

"Into the tepee! yelled Rea.

Jones plunged in after his comrade. The despairing howls of the dogs, drowned in more savage, frightful sounds, knelled one tragedy and foreboded a more terrible one. Jones looked out to see a white mass, like leaping waves of a rapid.

"Pump lead into thet!" cried Rea.

Rapidly Jones emptied his rifle into the white fray. The mass split; gaunt wolves leaped high to fall back dead; others wriggled and limped away; others dragged their hind quarters; others darted at the tepee.

"No more cartridges!" yelled Jones.

The giant grabbed the ax, and barred the door of the tepee. Crash! the heavy iron cleaved the skull of the first brute. Crash! it lamed the second. Then Rea stood in the narrow passage between the rocks, waiting with uplifted ax. A shaggy, white demon, snapping his jaws, sprang like a dog. A sodden, thudding blow met him and he slunk away without a cry. Another rabid beast launched his white body at the giant. Like a flash the ax descended. In agony the wolf fell, to spin round and round, running on his hind legs, while his head and shoulders and forelegs remained in the snow. His back was broken.

Jones crouched in the opening of the tepee, knife in hand. He doubted his senses. This was a nightmare. He saw two wolves leap at once. He heard the crash of the ax; he saw one wolf go down and the other slip under the swinging weapon to grasp the giant's hip. Jones's heard the rend of cloth, and then he pounced like a cat, to drive his knife into the body of the beast. Another nimble foe lunged at Rea, to sprawl broken and limp from the iron. It was a silent fight. The giant shut the way to his comrade and the calves; he made no outcry; he needed but one blow for every beast; magnificent, he wielded death and faced it—silent. He brought the white wild dogs of the north down with lightning blows, and when no more sprang to the attack, down on the frigid silence he rolled his cry: "Ho! Ho!"

"Rea! Rea! how is it with you?" called Jones, climbing out.

"A torn coat—no more, my lad."

Three of the poor dogs were dead; the fourth and last gasped at the hunters and died.

The wintry night became a thing of half-conscious past, a dream to the hunters, manifesting its reality only by the stark, stiff bodies of wolves, white in the gray morning.

"If we can eat, we'll make the cabin," said Rea. "But the dogs an' wolves are poison."

"Shall I kill a calf?" asked Jones.

"Ho! Ho! when hell freezes over—if we must!"

Jones found one 45–90 cartridge in all the outfit, and with that in the chamber of his rifle, once more struck south. Spruce trees began to show on the barrens and caribou trails roused hope in the hearts of the hunters.

"Look! in the spruces," whispered Jones, dropping the rope of his sled. Among the black trees gray objects moved.

"Caribou!" said Rea. "Hurry! Shoot! Don't miss!"

But Jones waited. He knew the value of the last bullet. He had a hunter's patience. When the caribou came out in an open space, Jones whistled. It was then the rifle grew set and fixed; it was then the red fire belched forth.

At four hundred yards the bullet took some fraction of time to strike. What a long time that was! Then both hunters heard the spiteful spat of the lead. The caribou fell, jumped up, ran down the slope, and fell again to rise no more.

An hour of rest, with fire and meat, changed the world to the hunters; still glistening, it yet had lost its bitter cold, its deathlike clutch.

"What's this?" cried Jones.

Moccasin tracks of different sizes, all toeing north, arrested the hunters.

"Pointed north! Wonder what thet means?" Rea plodded on, doubtfully shaking his head.

Night again, clear, cold, silver, starlit, silent night! The hunters rested, listening ever for the haunting mourn. Day again, white, passionless, monotonous, silent day! The hunters traveled on—on—on, ever listening for the haunting mourn.

Another dusk found them within thirty miles of their cabin. Only one more day now.

Rea talked of his furs, of the splendid white furs he could not bring. Jones talked of his little musk-oxen calves and joyfully watched them dig for moss in the snow.

Vigilance relaxed that night. Outworn nature rebelled, and both hunters slept.

Rea awoke first, and kicking off the blankets, went out. His terrible roar of rage made Jones fly to his side.

Under the very shadow of the tepee, where the little musk-oxen had been tethered, they lay stretched out pathetically on crimson snow—stiff stone-cold, dead. Moccasin tracks told the story of the tragedy.

Jones leaned against his comrade.

The giant raised his huge fist.

"Jackoway out of wood! Jackoway out of wood!"

Then he choked.

The north wind, blowing through the thin, dark, weird spruce trees, moaned and seemed to sigh, "Naza! Naza! Naza!"

11

On to the Siwash

"Who all was doin' the talkin' last night?" asked Frank next morning, when we were having a late breakfast. "Cause I've a joke on somebody. Jim he talks in his sleep often, an' last night after you did finally get settled down, Jim he up in his sleep an' says: 'Shore he's windy as hell! Shore he's windy as hell'!"

At this cruel exposure of his subjective wanderings, Jim showed extreme humiliation; but Frank's eyes fairly snapped with the fun he got out of telling it. The genial foreman loved a joke. The week's stay at Oak, in which we all became thoroughly acquainted, had presented Jim as always the same quiet character, easy, slow, silent, lovable. In his brother cowboy, however, we had discovered in addition to his fine, frank, friendly spirit, an overwhelming fondness for playing tricks. This boyish mischievousness, distinctly Arizonian, reached its acme whenever it tended in the direction of our serious leader.

Lawson had been dispatched on some mysterious errand about which my curiosity was all in vain. The order of the day was leisurely to get in readiness, and pack for our journey to the Siwash on the morrow. I watered my horse, played with the hounds, knocked about the cliffs, returned to the cabin, and lay down on my bed. Jim's hands were white with flour. He was kneading dough, and had several low, flat pans on the table. Wallace and Jones strolled in, and later Frank, and they all took various positions before the fire. I saw Frank, with the quickness of a sleight-of-hand performer, slip one of the pans of dough on the chair Jones had placed by the table. Jim did not see the action; Jones's and Wallace's backs were turned to Frank, and he did not know I was in the cabin. The conversation continued on the subject of Jones's big bay horse, which, hobbles and all, had gotten ten miles from camp the night before.

"Better count his ribs than his tracks," said Frank, and went on talking as easily and naturally as if he had not been expecting a very entertaining situation.

But no one could ever foretell Colonel Jones's actions. He showed every intention of seating himself in the chair, then walked over to his pack to begin searching for something or other. Wallace, however, promptly took the seat; and what began to be funnier than strange, he did not get up. Not unlikely this circumstance was owing to the fact that several of the rude chairs had soft layers of old blanket tacked on them. Whatever were Frank's internal emotions, he presented a remarkably placid and common-place exterior; but when Jim began to search for the missing pan of dough, the joker slowly sagged in his chair.

"Shore that beats hell!" said Jim. "I had three pans of dough. Could the pup have taken one?"

Wallace rose to his feet, and the bread pan clattered to the floor, with a clang and a clank, evidently protesting against the indignity it had suffered. But the dough stayed with Wallace, a great white conspicuous splotch on his corduroys. Jim, Frank and Jones all saw it at once.

"Why—Mr. Wal—lace—you set—in the dough!" exclaimed Frank, in a queer, strangled voice. Then he exploded, while Jim fell over the table.

It seemed that those two Arizona rangers, matured men though they were, would die of convulsions. I laughed with them, and so did Wallace, while he brought his bone-handled bowie knife into novel use. Buffalo Jones never cracked a smile, though he did remark about the waste of good flour.

Frank's face was a study for a psychologist when Jim actually apologized to Wallace for being so careless with his pans. I did not betray Frank, but I resolved to keep a still closer watch on him. It was partially because of this uneasy sense of his trickiness in the fringe of my mind that I made a discovery. My sleeping-bag rested on a raised platform in one corner, and at a favorable moment I examined the bag. It had not been tampered with, but I noticed a string running out through a chink between the logs. I found it came from a thick layer of straw under my bed, and had been tied to the end of a flatly coiled lasso. Leaving the thing as it was, I went outside and carelessly chased the hounds round the cabin. The string stretched along the logs to another chink, where it returned into the cabin at a point near where Frank slept. No great power of deduction was necessary to acquaint me with full details of the plot to spoil my slumbers. So I patiently awaited developments.

Lawson rode in near sundown with the carcasses of two beasts of some species hanging over his saddle. It turned out that Jones had planned a surprise for Wallace and me, and it could hardly have been a more enjoyable one, considering the time and place. We knew he had a flock of Persian sheep on the south slope of Buckskin, but had no idea it was within striking distance of Oak. Lawson had that day hunted up the shepherd and his sheep, to return to us with two sixty-pound Persian lambs. We feasted at supper-time on meat which was sweet, juicy, very tender and of as rare a flavor as that of the Rocky Mountain sheep.

My state after supper was one of huge enjoyment and with interest I awaited Frank's first spar for an opening. It came presently, in a lull of the conversation.

"Saw a big rattler run under the cabin to-day," he said, as if he were speaking of one of Old Buddy's shoes. "I tried to get a whack at him, but he oozed away too quick."

"Shore I seen him often," put in Jim. Good, old, honest Jim, led away by his trickster comrade! It was very plain. So I was to be frightened by snakes.

"These old cañon beds are ideal dens for rattlesnakes," chimed in my scientific California friend. "I have found several dens, but did not molest them as this is a particularly dangerous time of the year to meddle with the reptiles. Quite likely there's a den under the cabin."

While he made this remarkable statement, he had the grace to hide his face in a huge puff of smoke. He, too, was in the plot. I waited for Jones to come out with some ridiculous theory or fact concerning the particular species of snake, but as he did not speak, I concluded they had wisely left him out of the secret. After mentally debating a moment, I decided, as it was a very harmless joke, to help Frank to the fulfillment of his enjoyment.

"Rattlesnakes!" I exclaimed. "Heavens! I'd die if I heard one, let alone seeing it. A big rattler jumped at me one day, and I've never recovered from the shock."

Plainly, Frank was delighted to hear of any antipathy and my unfortunate experience, and he proceeded to expatiate on the viciousness of rattlesnakes, particularly those of Arizona. If I had believed the succeeding stories, emanating from the fertile brains of those three fellows, I should have made certain that Arizona cañons were Brazilian jungles. Frank's parting shot, sent in a mellow, kind voice, was the best point in the whole trick. "Now, I'd be nervous if I had a sleeping-bag like yours, because it's just the place for a rattler to ooze into."

In the confusion and dim light of bedtime I contrived to throw the end of my lasso over the horn of a saddle hanging on the wall, with the intention of augmenting the noise I soon expected to create; and I placed my automatic rifle and .38 S. and W. Special within easy reach of my hand. Then I crawled into my bag and composed myself to listen. Frank soon began to snore, so brazenly, so fictitiously, that I wondered at the man's absorbed intensity in his joke; and I was at great pains to smother in my breast a violent burst of riotous merriment. Jones's snores, however, were real enough, and this made me enjoy the situation all the more; because if he did not show a mild surprise when the catastrophe fell, I would greatly miss my guess. I knew the three wily conspirators were wide-awake. Suddenly I felt a movement in the straw under me and a faint rustling. It was so soft, so sinuous, that if I had not known it was the lasso, I would assuredly have been frightened. I gave a little jump, such as one will make quickly in bed. Then the coil ran out from under the straw.

How subtly suggestive of a snake! I made a slight outcry, a big jump, paused a moment for effectiveness—in which time Frank forgot to snore—then let out a tremendous yell, grabbed my guns, sent twelve thundering shots through the roof and pulled my lasso.

Crash! the saddle came down, to be followed by sounds not on Frank's programme and certainly not calculated upon by me. But they were all the more effective. I gathered that Lawson, who was not in the secret, and who was a nightmare sort of sleeper anyway, had knocked over Jim's table, with its array of pots and pans and then, unfortunately for Jones, had kicked that innocent person in the stomach.

As I lay there in my bag, the very happiest fellow in the wide world, the sound of my mirth was as the buzz of the wings of a fly to the mighty storm. Roar on roar filled the cabin.

When the three hypocrites recovered sufficiently from the startling climax to calm Lawson, who swore the cabin had been attacked by Indians; when Jones stopped roaring long enough to hear it was only a harmless snake that had caused the trouble, we hushed to repose once more—not, however, without hearing some trenchant remarks from the boiling Colonel anent fun and fools, and the indubitable fact that there was not a rattlesnake on Buckskin Mountain.

Long after this explosion had died away, I heard, or rather felt, a mysterious shudder or tremor of the cabin, and I knew that Frank and Jim were shaking with silent laughter. On my own score, I determined to find if Jones, in his strange make-up, had any sense of humor, or interest in life, or feeling, or love that did not center and hinge on four-footed beasts. In view of the rude awakening from what, no doubt, were pleasant dreams of wonderful white and green animals, combining the intelligence of man and strength of brutes—a new species creditable to his genius—I was perhaps unjust in my conviction as to his lack of humor. And as to the other question, whether or not he had any real human feeling for the creatures built in his own image, that was decided very soon and unexpectedly.

The following morning, as soon as Lawson got in with

the horses, we packed and started. Rather sorry was I to bid good-by to Oak Spring. Taking the back trail of the Stewarts, we walked the horses all day up a slowly narrowing, ascending cañon. The hounds crossed coyote and deer trails continually, but made no break. Sounder looked up as if to say he associated painful reminiscences with certain kinds of tracks. At the head of the cañon we reached timber at about the time dusk gathered, and we located for the night. Being once again nearly nine thousand feet high, we found the air bitterly cold, making a blazing fire most acceptable.

In the haste to get supper we all took a hand, and some one threw upon our tarpaulin tablecloth a tin cup of butter mixed with carbolic acid—a concoction Jones had used to bathe the sore feet of the dogs. Of course I got hold of this, spread a generous portion on my hot biscuit, placed some red-hot beans on that, and began to eat like a hungry hunter. At first I thought I was only burned. Then I recognized the taste and burn of the acid and knew something was wrong. Picking up the tin, I examined it, smelled the pungent odor, and felt a queer, numb sense of fear. This lasted only for a moment, as I well knew the use and power of the acid, and had not swallowed enough to hurt me. I was about to make known my mistake in a matter-of-fact way, when it flashed over me the accident could be made to serve a turn.

"Jones!" I cried hoarsely. "What's in this butter?"

"Lord! you haven't eaten any of that. Why, I put carbolic acid in it."

"Oh—oh—oh—oh I'm poisoned! I ate nearly all of it! Oh—I'm burning up! I'm dying!" With that I began to moan and rock to and fro and hold my stomach.

Consternation preceded shock. But in the excitement of the moment, Wallace—who, though badly scared, retained his wits—made for me with a can of condensed milk. He threw me back with no gentle hand, and was squeezing the life out of me to make me open my mouth, when I gave him a jab in his side. I imagined his surprise, as this peculiar reception of his first-aid-to-the-injured made him hold off to take a look at me, and in this interval I contrived to whisper to him: "Joke! Joke! you idiot! I'm only sham-ming. I want to see if I can scare Jones and get even with Frank. Help me out! Cry! Get tragic!"

From that moment I shall always believe that the stage lost a great tragedian in Wallace. With a magnificent gesture he threw the can of condensed milk at Jones, who was so stunned he did not try to dodge. "Thoughtless man! Murderer! it's too late!" cried Wallace, laying me back across his knees. "It's too late. His teeth are locked. He's far gone. Poor boy! poor boy! Who's to tell his mother?"

I could see from under my hat-brim that the solemn, hollow voice had penetrated the cold exterior of the plainsman. He could not speak; he clasped and unclasped his big hands in helpless fashion. Frank was as white as a sheet. This was simply delightful to me. But the expression of miserable, impotent distress on old Jim's sun-browned face was more than I could stand, and I could no longer keep up the deception. Just as Wallace cried out to Jones to pray—I wished then I had not weakened so soon—I got up and walked to the fire.

"Jim, I'll have another biscuit, please."

His under jaw dropped, then he nervously shoveled biscuits at me. Jones grabbed my hand and cried out with a voice that was new to me: "You can eat? You're better? You'll get over it?"

"Sure. Why, carbolic acid never phases me. I've often used it for rattlesnake bites. I did not tell you, but that rattler at the cabin last night actually bit me, and I used carbolic to cure the poison."

Frank mumbled something about horses, and faded into the gloom. As for Jones, he looked at me rather incredulously, and the absolute, almost childish gladness he manifested because I had been snatched from the grave, made me regret my deceit, and satisfied me forever on one score.

On awakening in the morning I found frost half an inch thick covered my sleeping-bag, whitened the ground, and made the beautiful silver spruce trees silver in hue as well as in name.

We were getting ready for an early start, when two

riders, with pack-horses jogging after them, came down the trail from the direction of Oak Spring. They proved to be Jeff Clarke, the wild-horse wrangler mentioned by the Stewarts, and his helper. They were on the way into the breaks for a string of pintos. Clarke was a short, heavily bearded man, of jovial aspect. He said he had met the Stewarts going into Fredonia, and being advised of our destination, had hurried to come up with us. As we did not know, except in a general way, where we were making for, the meeting was a fortunate event.

Our camping site had been close to the divide made by the one of the long, wooded ridges sent off by Buckskin Mountain, and soon we were descending again. We rode half a mile down a timbered slope, and then out into a beautiful, flat forest of gigantic pines. Clarke informed us it was a level bench some ten miles long, running out from the slopes of Buckskin to face the Grand Cañon on the south, and the breaks of the Siwash on the west. For two hours we rode between the stately lines of trees, and the hoofs of the horses gave forth no sound. A long, silvery grass, sprinkled with smiling bluebells, covered the ground, except close under the pines, where soft red mats invited lounging and rest. We saw numerous deer, great gray mule deer, almost as large as elk. Jones said they had been crossed with elk once, which accounted for their size. I did not see a stump, or a burned tree, or a windfall during the ride.

Clarke led us to the rim of the cañon. Without any preparation—for the giant trees hid the open sky—we rode right out to the edge of the tremendous chasm. At first I did not seem to think; my faculties were benumbed; only the pure sensorial instinct of the savage who sees, but does not feel, made me take note of the abyss. Not one of our party had ever seen the cañon from this side, and not one of us said a word. But Clarke kept talking.

"Wild place this is hyar," he said. "Seldom any one but horse wranglers gits over this far. I've bed a bunch of wild pintos down in a cañon below fer two years. I reckon you can't find no better place fer camp than right hyar. Listen. Do you hear thet rumble? Thet's Thunder Falls. You can only see it from one place, an' thet far off, but thar's brooks you can git at to water the hosses. Fer thet matter, you can ride up the slopes an' git snow. If you can git snow close, it'd be better, fer thet's an all-fired bad trail down fer water."

"Is this the cougar country the Stewarts talked about?" asked Jones.

"Reckon it is. Cougars is as thick in hyar as rabbits in a spring-hole cañon. I'm on the way now to bring up my pintos. The cougars hev cost me hundreds—I might say thousands of dollars. I lose hosses all the time; an' damn me, gentlemen, I've never raised a colt. This is the greatest cougar country in the West. Look at those yellow crags! Thar's where the cougars stay. No one ever hunted 'em. It seems to me they can't be hunted. Deer and wild hosses by the thousand browse hyar on the mountain in summer, an' down in the breaks in winter. The cougars live fat. You'll find deer and wild-hoss carcasses all over this country. You'll find lions's dens full of bones. You'll find warm deer left for the coyotes. But whether you'll find the cougars, I can't say. I fetched dogs in hyar, an' tried to ketch Old Tom. I've put them on his trail an' never saw hide nor hair of them again. Jones, it's no easy huntin' hyar."

"Well, I can see that," replied our leader. "I never hunted lions in such a country, and never knew any one who had. We'll have to learn how. We've the time and the dogs, all we need is the stuff in us."

"I hope you fellars git some cougars, an' I believe you will. Whatever you do, kill Old Tom."

"We'll catch him alive. We're not on a hunt to kill cougars," said Jones.

"What!" exclaimed Clarke, looking from Jones to us. His rugged face wore a half-smile.

"Jones ropes cougars, an' ties them up," replied Frank.

"I'm—— ——if he'll ever rope Old Tom," burst out Clarke, ejecting a huge quid of tobacco. "Why, man alive! it'd be the death of you to git near thet old villain. I never seen him, but I've seen his tracks fer five years. They're larger than any hoss tracks you ever seen. He'll weigh over three hundred, thet old cougar. Hyar, take a look at my man's hoss. Look at his back. See them marks? Wal, Old Tom made them, an' he made them right in camp last fall, when we were down in the cañon."

The mustang to which Clarke called our attention was a sleek cream and white pinto. Upon his side and back were long regular scars, some an inch wide, and bare of hair.

"How on earth did he get rid of the cougar?" asked Jones.

"I don't know. Perhaps he got scared of the dogs. It took thet pinto a year to git well. Old Tom is a real lion. He'll kill a full-grown hoss when he wants, but a yearlin' colt is his especial likin'. You're sure to run acrost his trail, an' you'll never miss it. Wal, if I find any cougar sign down in the cañon, I'll build two fires so as to let you know. Though no hunter, I'm tolerably acquainted with the varmints. The deer an' hosses are rangin' the forest slopes now, an' I think the cougars come up over the rim rock at night an' go back in the mornin'. Anyway, if your dogs can follow the trails, you've got sport, an' more'n sport comin' to you. But take it from me—don't try to rope Old Tom."

After all our disappointments in the beginning of the expedition, our hardship on the desert, our trials with the dogs and horses, it was real pleasure to make permanent camp with wood, water and feed at hand, a soul-stirring, ever-changing picture before us, and the certainty that we were in the wild lairs of the lions—among the Lords of the Crags!

While we were unpacking, every now and then I would straighten up and gaze out beyond. I knew the outlook was magnificent and sublime beyond words, but as yet I had not begun to understand it. The great pine trees, growing to the very edge of the rim, received their full quota of appreciation from me, as did the smooth, flower-decked aisles leading back into the forest.

The location we selected for camp was a large glade, fifty paces or more from the precipice—far enough, the cowboys averred, to keep our traps from being sucked down by some of the whirlpool winds, native to the spot. In the center of this glade stood a huge gnarled and blasted old pine, that certainly by virtue of hoary locks and bent shoulders had earned the right to stand aloof from his younger companions. Under this tree we placed all our belongings, and then, as Frank so felicitously expressed it, we were free to "ooze round an' see things."

I believe I had a sort of subconscious, selfish idea that some one would steal the cañon away from me if I did not hurry to make it mine forever; so I sneaked off, and sat under a pine growing on the very rim. At first glance, I saw below me, seemingly miles away, a wild chaos of red and buff mesas rising out of dark purple clefts. Beyond these reared a long, irregular tableland, running south almost to the extent of my vision, which I remembered Clarke had called Powell's Plateau. I remembered, also, that he had said it was twenty miles distant, was almost that many miles long, was connected to the mainland of Buckskin Mountain by a very narrow wooded dip of land called the Saddle, and that it practically shut us out of a view of the Grand Cañon proper. If that was true, what, then, could be the name of the cañon at my feet? Suddenly, as my gaze wandered from point to point, it was arrested by a dark, conical mountain, white-tipped, which rose in the notch of the Saddle. What could it mean? Were there such things as cañon mirages? Then the dim purple of its color told of its great distance from me; and then its familiar shape told I had come into my own again—I had found my old friend once more. For in all that plateau there was only one snow-capped mountain—the San Francisco Peak; and there, a hundred and fifty, perhaps two hundred miles away, far beyond the Grand Cañon, it smiled brightly at me, as it had for days and days across the desert.

Hearing Jones yelling for somebody or everybody, I jumped up to find a procession heading for a point farther down the rim wall, where our leader stood waving his arms. The excitement proved to have been caused by cougar signs at the head of the trail where Clarke had started down.

"They're here, boys, they're here," Jones kept repeating, as he showed us different tracks. "This sign is not so old. Boys, to-morrow we'll get up a lion, sure as you're born. And if we do, and Sounder sees him, then we've got a lion-dog! I'm afraid of Don. He has a fine nose; he can run and fight, but he's been trained to deer, and maybe I can't break him. Moze is still uncertain. If old Jude only hadn't been lamed! She would be the best of the lot. But Sounder is our hope. I'm almost ready to swear by him."

All this was too much for me, so I slipped off again to be alone, and this time headed for the forest. Warm patches of sunlight, like gold, brightened the ground; dark patches of sky, like ocean blue, gleamed between the treetops. Hardly a rustle of wind in the fine-toothed green branches disturbed the quiet. When I got fully out of sight of camp, I started to run as if I were a wild Indian. My running had no aim; just sheer mad joy of the grand old forest, the smell of pine, the wild silence of beauty loosed the spirit in me so it had to run, and I ran with it till the physical being failed.

While resting on a fragrant bed of pine needles, endeavoring to regain control over a truant mind, trying to subdue the encroaching of the natural man on the civilized man, I saw gray objects moving under the trees. I lost them, then saw them, and presently so plainly that, with delight on delight, I counted seventeen deer pass through an open arch of dark green. Rising to my feet, I ran to get round a low mound. They saw me and bounded away with prodigiously long leaps. Bringing their forefeet together, stiff-legged under them, they bounced high, like rubber balls, yet they were graceful.

The forest was so open that I could watch them for a long way; and as I circled with my gaze, a glimpse of something white arrested my attention. A light, grayish animal appeared to be tearing at an old stump. Upon nearer view, I recognized a wolf, and he scented or sighted me at the same moment, and loped off into the shadows of the trees. Approaching the spot where I had marked him I found he had been feeding from the carcass of a horse. The remains had been only partly eaten, and were of an animal of the mustang build that had evidently been recently killed. Frightful lacerations under the throat showed where a lion had taken fatal hold. Deep furrows in the ground proved how the mustang had sunk his hoofs, reared and shaken himself. I traced roughly defined tracks fifty paces to the lee of a little bank, from which I concluded the lion had sprung.

I gave free rein to my imagination and saw the forest dark, silent, peopled by none but its savage denizens. The lion crept like a shadow, crouched noiselessly down, then leaped on his sleeping or browsing prey. The lonely night stillness split to a frantic snort and scream of terror, and the stricken mustang with his mortal enemy upon his back, dashed off with fierce, wild love of life. As he went he felt his foe crawl toward his neck on claws of fire; he saw the tawny body and the gleaming eyes; then the cruel teeth snapped with the sudden bite, and the woodland tragedy ended.

On the spot I conceived an antipathy toward lions. It was born of the frightful spectacle of what had once been a glossy, prancing mustang, of the mute, sickening proof of the survival of the fittest, of the law that levels life.

Upon telling my camp-fellows about my discovery, Jones and Wallace walked out to see it, while Jim told me the wolf I had seen was a "lofer," one of the giant buffalo wolves of Buckskin; and if I would watch the carcass in the mornings and evenings, I would "shore as hell get a plunk at him."

White pine burned in a beautiful, clear blue flame, with no smoke; and in the center of the campfire left a golden heart. But Jones would not have any sitting up, and hustled us off to bed, saying we would be "blamed" glad of it in about fifteen hours. I crawled into my sleeping-bag, made a hood of my Navajo blanket, and peeping from under it, watched the fire and the flickering shadows. The blaze burned down rapidly. Then the stars blinked. Arizona stars would be moons in any other State! How serene, peaceful, august, infinite and wonderfully bright! No breeze stirred the pines. The clear tinkle of the cowbells on the hobbled horses rang from near and distant parts of the forest. The prosaic bell of the meadow and the pasture brook, here, in this environment, jingled out different notes, as clear, sweet, musical as silver bells.

12

Old Tom

A t daybreak our leader routed us out. The frost mantled the ground so heavily that it looked like snow, and the rare atmosphere bit like the breath of winter. The forest stood solemn and gray; the cañon lay wrapped in vapory slumber.

Hot biscuits and coffee, with a chop or two of the delicious Persian lamb meat, put a less Spartan tinge on the morning, and gave Wallace and me more strength—we needed not incentive—to leave the fire, hustle our saddles on the horses and get in line with our impatient leader. The hounds scampered over the frost, shoving their noses at the tufts of grass and bluebells. Lawson and Jim remained in camp; and the rest of us trooped southwest.

A mile or so in that direction, the forest of pine ended abruptly, and a wide belt of low, scrubby oak trees, breast high to a horse, fringed the rim of the cañon and appeared to broaden out and grow wavy southward. The edge of the forest was as dark and regular as if a band of woodchoppers had trimmed it. We threaded our way through this thicket, all peering into the bisecting deer trails for cougar tracks in the dust.

"Bring the dogs! Hurry!" suddenly called Jones from a thicket.

We lost no time complying, and found him standing in a trail, with his eyes on the sand. "Take a look, boys. A

131

good-sized male cougar passed here last night. Hyar, Sounder, Don, Moze, come on!"

It was a nervous, excited pack of hounds. Old Jude got to Jones first, and she sang out; then Sounder opened with his ringing bay, and before Jones could mount, a string of yelping dogs sailed straight for the forest.

"Ooze along boys!" yelled Frank, wheeling Spot.

With the cowboy leading, we strung into the pines, and I found myself behind. Presently even Wallace disappeared. I almost threw the reins at Satan, and yelled for him to go. The result enlightened me. Like an arrow from a bow, the black shot forward. Frank had told me of his speed, that when he found his stride it was like riding a flying feather to be on him. Jones, fearing he would kill me, had cautioned me always to hold him in, which I had done. Satan stretched out with long, graceful motions; he did not turn aside for logs, but cleared them with easy and powerful spring, and he swerved only slightly for the trees. This latter, I saw at once, made the danger for me. It became a matter of saving my legs, and dodging branches. The imperative need of this came to me with convincing force. I dodged a branch on one tree, only to be caught square in the middle by a snag on another. Crack! If the snag had not broken, Satan would have gone on riderless, and I would have been left hanging, a pathetic and drooping monition to the risks of the hunt. I kept ducking my head, now and then falling flat over the pommel to avoid a limb that would have brushed me off, and hugging the flanks of my horse with my knees. Soon I was at Wallace's heels, and had Jones in sight. Now and then glimpses of Frank's white horse gleamed through the trees.

We began to circle toward the south, to go up and down shallow hollows, to find the pines thinning out; then we shot out of the forest into the scrubby oak. Riding through this brush was the cruelest kind of work, but Satan kept on close to the sorrel. The hollows began to get deeper, and the ridges between them narrower. No longer could we keep a straight course.

On the crest of one of the ridges we found Jones

awaiting us. Jude, Tige and Don lay panting at his feet. Plainly the Colonel appeared vexed.

"Listen," he said, when we reined in.

We complied, but did not hear a sound.

"Frank's beyond there some place," continued Jones, "but I can't see him, nor hear the hounds any more. Don and Tige split again on deer trails. Old Jude hung on the lion track, but I stopped her here. There's something I can't figure. Moze held a beeline southwest, and he yelled seldom. Sounder gradually stopped baying. Maybe Frank can tell us something."

Jones's long drawn-out signal was answered from the direction he expected, and after a little time, Frank's white horse shone out of the gray-green of a ridge a mile away.

This drew my attention to our position. We were on a high ridge out in the open, and I could see fifty miles of the shaggy slopes of Buckskin. Southward the gray, ragged line seemed to stop suddenly, and beyond it purple haze hung over a void I knew to be the cañon. And facing west, I came, at last, to understand perfectly the meaning of the breaks in the Siwash. They were nothing more than ravines that headed up on the slopes and ran down, getting deeper and steeper, though scarcely wider, to break into the cañon. Knife-crested ridges rolled westward, wave on wave, like the billows of a sea. I appreciated that these breaks were, at their sources, little washes easy to jump across, and at their mouths a mile deep and impassable. Huge pine trees shaded these gullies, to give way to the gray growth of stunted oak, which in turn merged into the dark green of piñon. A wonderful country for deer and lions, it seemed to me, but impassable, all but impassable for a hunter.

Frank soon appeared, brushing through the bending oaks, and Sounder trotted along behind him.

"Where's Moze?" inquired Jones.

"The last I heard of Moze he was out of the brush, goin' across the piñon flat, right for the cañon. He had a hot trail."

"Well, we're certain of one thing; if it was a deer, he won't come back soon, and if it was a lion, he'll tree it, lose the scent, and come back. We've got to show the hounds a lion in a tree. They'd run a hot trail, bump into a tree, and then be at fault. What was wrong with Sounder?"

"I don't know. He came back to me."

"We can't trust him, or any of them yet. Still, maybe they're doing better than we know."

The outcome of the chase, so favorably started was a disappointment, which we all felt keenly. After some discussion, we turned south, intending to ride down to the rim wall and follow it back to camp. I happened to turn once, perhaps to look again at the far-distant pink cliffs of Utah, or the wave-like dome of Trumbull Mountain, when I saw Moze trailing close behind me. My yell halted the Colonel.

"Well, I'll be darned!" ejaculated he, as Moze hove in sight. "Come hyar, you rascal!"

He was a tired dog, but had no sheepish air about him, such as he had worn when lagging in from deer chases. He wagged his tail, and flopped down to pant and pant, as if to say: "What's wrong with you guys?"

"Boys, for two cents I'd go back and put Jude on that trail. It's just possible that Moze treed a lion. But—well, I expect there's more likelihood of his chasing the lion over the rim; so we may as well keep on. The strange thing is that Sounder wasn't with Moze. There may have been two lions. You see we are up a tree ourselves. I have known lions to run in pairs, and also a mother keep four two-year-olds with her. But such cases are rare. Here, in this country, though, maybe they run round and have parties."

As we left the breaks behind we got out upon a level piñon flat. A few cedars grew with the piñons. Deer runways and trails were thick.

"Boys, look at that," said Jones. "This is great lion country, the best I ever saw."

He pointed to the sunken, red, shapeless remains of two horses, and near them a ghastly scattering of bleached bones. "A lion-lair right here on the flat. Those two horses were killed early this spring, and I see no signs of their carcasses having been covered with brush and dirt. I've got to learn lion lore over again, that's certain."

As we paused at the head of a depression, which appeared to be a gap in the rim wall, filled with massed piñons and splintered piles of yellow stone, I caught Sounder going through some interesting moves. He stopped to smell a bush. Then he lifted his head, and electrified me with a great, deep-sounding bay.

"Hi! there, listen to that!" yelled Jones. "What's Sounder got? Give him room—don't run him down. Easy now, old dog, easy, easy!"

Sounder suddenly broke down a trail. Moze howled, Don barked, and Tige let out his staccato yelp. They ran through the brush here, there, everywhere. Then all at once old Jude chimed in with her mellow voice, and Jones tumbled off his horse.

"By the Lord Harry! There's something there."

"Here, Colonel, here's the bush Sounder smelt, and there's a sandy trail under it," I called.

"There go Don an' Tige down into the break," cried Frank. "They've got a hot scent!"

Jones stooped over the place I designated, to jerk up with reddening face, and as he flung himself into the saddle roared out: "After Sounder! Old Tom! Old Tom! Old Tom!"

We all heard Sounder, and at the moment of Jones's discovery, Moze got the scent and plunged ahead of us.

"Hi! Hi! Hi! Hi!" yelled the Colonel. Frank sent Spot forward like a white streak. Sounder called to us in irresistible bays, which Moze answered, and then crippled Jude bayed in baffled, impotent distress.

The atmosphere was charged with that lion. As if by magic, the excitation communicated itself to all, and men, horses and dogs acted in accord. The ride through the forest had been a jaunt. This was a steeplechase, a mad, heedless, perilous, glorious race. And we had for a pacemaker a cowboy mounted on a tireless mustang.

Always it seemed to me, while the wind rushed, the brush whipped, I saw Frank far ahead, sitting his saddle as if glued there, holding his reins loosely forward. To see him ride so was a beautiful sight. Jones let out his Comanche yell at every dozen jumps, and Wallace sent back a thrilling "Waa-hoo-o!" In the excitement I had again checked my horse, and when I remembered, and loosed the bridle, how the noble animal responded! The pace he settled into dazed me; I could hardly distinguish the deer trail down which he was thundering. I lost my comrades ahead; the piñon blurred in my sight; I only faintly heard the hounds. It occurred to me we were making for the breaks, but I did not think of checking Satan. I thought only of flying on faster and faster.

"On! On! old fellow! Stretch out! Never lose this race! We've got to be there at the finish!" I called to Satan, and he seemed to understand and stretched lower, farther, quicker.

The brush pounded my legs and clutched and tore my clothes; the wind whistled; the piñon branches cut and whipped my face. Once I dodged to the left, as Satan swerved to the right, with the result that I flew out of the saddle, and crashed into a piñon tree, which marvelously brushed me back into the saddle. The wild yells and deep bays sounded nearer. Satan tripped and plunged down, throwing me as gracefully as an aërial tumbler wings his flight. I alighted in a bush, without feeling of scratch or pain. As Satan recovered and ran past, I did not seek to make him stop, but getting a good grip on the pommel, I vaulted up again. Once more he raced like a wild mustang. And from nearer and nearer in front pealed the alluring sounds of the chase.

Satan was creeping close to Wallace and Jones, with Frank looming white through the occasional piñons. Then all dropped out of sight, to appear again suddenly. They had reached the first break. Soon I was upon it. Two deer ran out of the ravine, almost brushing my horse in the haste. Satan went down and up in a few giant strides. Only the narrow ridge separated us from another break. It was up and down then for Satan, a work to which he manfully set himself. Occasionally I saw Wallace and Jones, but heard them oftener. All the time the breaks grew deeper, till finally Satan had to zigzag his way down and up. Discouragement fastened on me, when from the summit of the next ridge I saw Frank far down the break, with Jones and Wallace not a quarter of a mile away from him. I sent out a long, exultant yell as Satan crushed into the hard, dry wash in the bottom of the break.

I knew from the way he quickened under me that he intended to overhaul somebody. Perhaps because of the clear going, or because my frenzy had cooled to a thrilling excitement which permitted detail, I saw clearly and distinctly the speeding horsemen down the ravine. I picked out the smooth pieces of ground ahead, and with the slightest touch of the rein on his neck, guided Satan into them. How he ran! The light, quick beats of his hoofs were regular, pounding. Seeing Jones and Wallace sail high into the air, I knew they had jumped a ditch. Thus prepared, I managed to stick on when it yawned before me; and Satan, never slackening, leaped up and up, giving me a new swing.

Dust began to settle in little clouds before me; Frank, far ahead, had turned his mustang up the side of the break; Wallace, within hailing distance, now turned to wave me a hand. The rushing wind fairly sang in my ears; the walls of the break were confused blurs of yellow and green; at every stride Satan seemed to swallow a rod of the white trail.

Jones began to scale the ravine, heading up obliquely far on the side of where Frank had vanished, and as Wallace followed suit, I turned Satan. I caught Wallace at the summit, and we raced together out upon another flat of piñon. We heard Frank and Jones yelling in a way that caused us to spur our horses frantically. Spot, gleaming white near a clump of green piñons, was our guiding star. That last quarter of a mile was a ringing run, a ride to remember.

As our mounts crashed back with stiff forelegs and haunches, Wallace and I leaped off and darted into the clump of piñons, whence issued a hair-raising medley of yells and barks. I saw Jones, then Frank, both waving their arms, then Moze and Sounder running wildly, aimlessly about.

"Look there!" rang in my ear, and Jones smashed me on the back with a blow, which at any ordinary time would have laid me flat.

In a low, stubby piñon tree, scarce twenty feet from us,

was a tawny form. An enormous mountain-lion, as large as an African lioness, stood planted with huge, round legs on two branches; and he faced us gloomily, neither frightened nor fierce. He watched the running dogs with pale, yellow eyes, waved his massive head and switched his long, black-tufted tail.

"It's Old Tom! sure as you're born! It's Old Tom!" yelled Jones. "There's no two lions like that in one country. Hold still now. Jude is here, and she'll see him—she'll show him to the other hounds. Hold still!"

We heard Jude coming at a fast pace for a lame dog, and we saw her presently, running with her nose down for a moment, then up. She entered the clump of trees, and bumped her nose against the piñon Old Tom was in, and looked up like a dog that knew her business. The series of wild howls she broke into quickly brought Sounder and Moze to her side. They, too, saw the big lion, not fifteen feet over their heads.

We were all yelling and trying to talk at once, in some such state as the dogs.

"Hyar, Moze! Come down out of that!" hoarsely shouted Jones.

Moze had begun to climb the thick, many-branched, low piñon tree. He paid not the slightest attention to Jones, who screamed and raged at him.

"Cover the lion!" cried he to me. "Don't shoot unless he crouches to jump on me."

The little beaded front-sight wavered slightly as I held my rifle leveled at the grim, snarling face, and out of the corner of my eye, as it were, I saw Jones dash in under the lion and grasp Moze by the hind leg and haul him down. He broke from Jones and leaped again to the first low branch. His master then grasped his collar and carried him to where we stood and held him choking.

"Boys, we can't keep Tom up there. When he jumps, keep out of his way. Maybe we can chase him up a better tree."

Old Tom suddenly left the branches, swinging violently; and hitting the ground like a huge cat on springs, he bounded off, tail up, in a most ludicrous manner. His running, however, did not lack speed, for he quickly outdistanced the bursting hounds.

A stampede for horses succeeded this move. I had difficulty in closing my camera, which I had forgotten until the last moment, and got behind the others. Satan sent the dust flying and the piñon branches crashing. Hardly had I time to bewail my ill-luck in being left, when I dashed out of a thick growth of trees to come upon my companions, all dismounted on the rim of the Grand Cañon.

"He's gone down! He's gone down!" raged Jones, stamping the ground. "What luck! What miserable luck! But don't quit; spread along the rim, boys, and look for him. Cougars can't fly. There's a break in the rim somewhere."

The rock wall, on which we dizzily stood, dropped straight down for a thousand feet, to meet a long, piñon-covered slope, which graded a mile to cut off into what must have been the second wall. We were far west of Clarke's trail now, and faced a point above where Kanab Cañon, a red gorge a mile deep, met the great cañon. As I ran along the rim, looking for a fissure or break, my gaze seemed impellingly drawn by the immensity of this thing I could not name, and for which I had as yet no intelligible emotion.

Two "Waa-hoos" in the rear turned me back in double-quick time, and hastening by the horses, I found the three men grouped at the head of a narrow break.

"He went down here. Wallace saw him round the base of that tottering crag."

The break was wedged-shaped, with the sharp end toward the rim, and it descended so rapidly as to appear almost perpendicular. It was a long steep slide of small, weathered shale, and a place that no man in his right senses would ever have considered going down. But Jones, designating Frank and me, said in his cool, quick voice:

"You fellows go down. Take Jude and Sounder in leash. If you find his trail below along the wall, yell for us. Meanwhile, Wallace and I will hang over the rim and watch for him."

Going down, in one sense, was much easier than had appeared, for the reason that once started we moved on sliding beds of weathered stone. Each of us now had an avalanche for a steed. Frank forged ahead with a roar, and then seeing danger below, tried to get out of the mass. But the stones were like quicksand; every step he took sank him in deeper. He grasped the smooth cliff, to find holding impossible. The slide poured over a fall like so much water. He reached and caught a branch of a piñon, and lifting his feet up, hung on till the treacherous area of moving stones had passed.

While I had been absorbed in his predicament, my avalanche augmented itself by slide on slide, perhaps loosened by his; and before I knew it, I was sailing down with ever-increasing momentum. The sensation was distinctly pleasant, and a certain spirit, before restrained in me, at last ran riot. The slide narrowed at the drop where Frank had jumped, and the stones poured over in a stream. I jumped also, but having a rifle in one hand, failed to hold, and plunged down into the slide again. My feet were held this time, as in a vise. I kept myself upright and waited. Fortunately, the jumble of loose stone slowed and stopped, enabling me to crawl over to one side where there was comparatively good footing. Below us, for fifty yards, was a sheet of rough stone, as bare as washed granite well could be. We slid down this in regular schoolboy fashion, and had reached another restricted neck in the fissure, when a sliding crash above warned us that the avalanches had decided to move of their own free will. Only a fraction of a moment had we to find footing along the yellow cliff, when, with a cracking roar, the mass struck the slippery granite. If we had been on that slope, our lives would not have been worth a grain of the dust flying in clouds above us. Huge stones, that had formed the bottom of the slides, shot ahead, and rolling, leaping, whizzed by us with frightful velocity, and the remainder groaned and growled its way down, to thunder over the second fall and die out in a distant rumble.

The hounds had hung back, and were not easily coaxed down to us. From there on, down to the base of the gigantic cliff, we descended with little difficulty.

"We might meet the old gray cat anywheres along here," said Frank.

The wall of yellow limestone had shelves, ledges, fissures and cracks, any one of which might have concealed a lion. On these places I turned dark, uneasy glances. It seemed to me events succeeded one another so rapidly that I had no time to think, to examine, to prepare. We were rushed from one sensation to another.

"Gee! look here," said Frank; "here's his tracks. Did you ever see the like of that?"

Certainly I had never fixed my eyes on such enormous cat-tracks as appeared in the yellow dust at the base of the rim wall. The mere sight of them was sufficient to make a man tremble.

"Hold in the dogs, Frank," I called. "Listen. I think I heard a yell."

From far above came a yell, which, though thinned out by distance, was easily recognized as Jones's. We returned to the opening of the break, and throwing our heads back, looked up the slide to see him coming down.

"Wait for me! Wait for me! I saw the lion go in a cave. Wait for me!"

With the same roar and crack and slide of rocks as had attended our descent, Jones bore down on us. For an old man it was a marvelous performance. He walked on the avalanches as though he wore seven-league boots, and presently, as we began to dodge whizzing bowlders, he stepped down to us, whirling his coiled lasso. His jaw bulged out; a flash made fire in his cold eyes.

"Boys, we've got Old Tom in a corner. I worked along the rim north and looked over every place I could. Now, maybe you won't believe it, but I heard him pant. Yes, sir, he panted like the tired lion he is. Well, presently I saw him lying along the base of the rim wall. His tongue was hanging out. You see, he's a heavy lion, and not used to running long distances. Come on, now. It's not far. Hold in the dogs. You there with the rifle, lead off, and keep your eyes peeled."

Single file, we passed along in the shadow of the great cliff. A wide trail had been worn in the dust.

"A lion run-way," said Jones. "Don't you smell the cat?"

Indeed, the strong odor of cat was very pronounced; and that, without the big fresh tracks, made the skin on my face tighten and chill. As we turned a jutting point in the wall, a number of animals, which I did not recognize, plunged helter-skelter down the cañon slope.

"Rocky Mountain sheep!" exclaimed Jones. "Look! Well, this is a discovery. I never heard of a bighorn in the cañon."

It was indicative of the strong grip Old Tom had on us that we at once forgot the remarkable fact of coming upon those rare sheep in such a place.

Jones halted us presently before a deep curve described by the rim wall, the extreme end of which terminated across the slope in an impassable projecting corner.

"See across there, boys. See that black hole. Old Tom's in there."

"What's your plan?" queried the cowboy sharply.

"Wait. We'll slip up to get better lay of the land."

We worked our way noiselessly along the rim-wall curve for several hundred yards and came to a halt again, this time with a splendid command of the situation. The trail ended abruptly at the dark cave, so menacingly staring at us, and the corner of the cliff had curled back upon itself. It was a box-trap, with a drop at the end, too great for any beast, a narrow slide of weathered stone running down, and the rim wall trail. Old Tom would plainly be compelled to choose one of these directions if he left his cave.

"Frank, you and I will keep to the wall and stop near that scrub piñon, this side of the hole. If I rope him, I can use that tree."

Then he turned to me:

"Are you to be depended on here?"

"I? What do you want me to do?" I demanded, and my whole breast seemed to sink in.

"You cut across the head of this slope and take up your position in the slide below the cave, say just by that big stone. From there you can command the cave, our position and your own. Now, if it is necessary to kill this lion to save me or Frank, or, of course, yourself, can you be depended upon to kill him?"

I felt a queer sensation around my heart and a strange tightening of the skin upon my face! What a position for me to be placed in! For one instant I shook like a quivering aspen leaf. Then because of the pride of a man, or perhaps inherited instincts cropping out at this perilous moment, I looked up and answered quietly:

"Yes. I will kill him!"

"Old Tom is cornered, and he'll come out. He can run only two ways: along this trail, or down that slide. I'll take my stand by the scrub piñon there so I can get a hitch if I rope him. Frank, when I give the word, let the dogs go. Grey, you block the slide. If he makes at us, even if I do get my rope on him, kill him! Most likely he'll jump down hill—then you'll *have* to kill him! Be quick. Now loose the hounds. Hi! Hi! Hi! Hi!"

I jumped into the narrow slide of weathered stone and looked up. Jones's stentorian yell rose high above the clamor of the hounds. He whirled his lasso.

A huge yellow form shot over the trail and hit the top of the slide with a crash. The lasso streaked out with arrowy swiftness, circled, and snapped viciously close to Old Tom's head. "Kill him! Kill him!" roared Jones. Then the lion leaped, seemingly into the air above me. Instinctively I raised my little automatic rifle. I seemed to hear a million bellowing reports. The tawny body, with its grim, snarling face, blurred in my sight. I heard a roar of sliding stones at my feet. I felt a rush of wind. I caught a confused glimpse of a whirling wheel of fur, rolling down the slide.

Then Jones and Frank were pounding me, and yelling I know not what. From far above came floating down a long "Waa-hoo!" I saw Wallace silhouetted against the blue sky. I felt the hot barrel of my rifle, and shuddered at the bloody stones below me—then, and then only, did I realize, with weakening legs, that Old Tom had jumped at me, and had jumped to his death.

13

Singing Cliffs

Old Tom had rolled two hundred yards down the
cañon, leaving a red trail and bits of fur behind him.
When I had clambered down to the steep slide
where he had lodged, Sounder and Jude had just decided
he was no longer worth biting, and were wagging their tails.
Frank was shaking his head, and Jones, standing above the
lion, lasso in hand, wore a disconsolate face.

"How I wish I had got the rope on him!"

"I reckon we'd be gatherin' up the pieces of you if you
had," said Frank, dryly.

We skinned the old king on the rocky slope of his
mighty throne, and then, beginning to feel the effects of
severe exertion, we cut across the slope for the foot of the
break. Once there, we gazed up in dismay. That break
resembled a walk of life—how easy to slip down, how hard
to climb! Even Frank, inured as he was to strenuous toil,
began to swear and wipe his sweaty brow before we had
made one-tenth of the ascent. It was particularly exasperating, not to mention the danger of it, to work a few feet up
a slide, and then feel it start to move. We had to climb in
single file, which jeopardized the safety of those behind the
leader. Sometimes we were all sliding at once, like boys on
a pond, with the difference that we were in danger. Frank
forged ahead, turning to yell now and then for us to dodge
a cracking stone. Faithful old Jude could not get up in some
places, so laying aside my rifle, I carried her, and returned

144

for the weapon. It became necessary, presently, to hide behind cliff projections to escape the avalanches started by Frank, and to wait till he had surmounted the break. Jones gave out completely several times, saying the exertion affected his heart. What with my rifle, my camera and Jude, I could offer him no assistance, and was really in need of that myself. When it seemed as if one more step would kill us, we reached the rim, and fell panting with labored chests and dripping skins. We could not speak. Jones had worn a pair of ordinary shoes without thick soles and nails, and it seemed well to speak of them in the past tense. They were split into ribbons and hung on by the laces. His feet were cut and bruised.

On the way back to camp, we encountered Moze and Don coming out of the break where we had started Sounder on the trail. The paws of both hounds were yellow with dust, which proved they had been down under the rim wall. Jones doubted not in the least that they had chased a lion.

Upon examination, this break proved to be one of the two which Clarke used for trails to his wild horse corral in the cañon. According to him, the distance separating them was five miles by the rim wall, and less than half that in a straight line. Therefore, we made for the point of the forest where it ended abruptly in the scrub oak. We got into camp, a fatigued lot of men, horses and dogs. Jones appeared particularly happy, and his first move, after dismounting, was to stretch out the lion skin and measure it.

"Ten feet, three inches and a half!" he said with pride.

"Shore it do beat hell!" exclaimed Jim in tones nearer to excitement than any I had ever heard him use.

"Old Tom beats, by two inches, any cougar I ever saw," continued Jones. "He must have weighed more than three hundred. We'll set about curing the hide. Jim, stretch it well on a tree, and we'll take a hand in peeling off the fat."

All of the party worked on the cougar skin that afternoon. The gristle at the base of the neck, where it met the shoulders, was so tough and thick we could not scrape it thin. Jones said this particular spot was so well protected

because in fighting, cougars were most likely to bite and
claw there. For that matter, the whole skin was tough,
tougher than leather; and when it dried, it pulled all the
horseshoe nails out of the pine tree upon which we had it
stretched.

About time for the sun to set, I strolled along the rim
wall to look into the cañon. I was beginning to feel
something of its character and had growing impressions.
Dark purple smoke veiled the clefts deep down between
the mesas. I walked along to where points of cliff ran out
like capes and peninsulas, all seamed, cracked, wrinkled,
scarred and yellow with age, with shattered, topping ruins
of rocks ready at a touch to go thundering down. I could not
resist the temptation to crawl out to the farthest point, even
though I shuddered over the yard-wide ridges; and when
once seated on a bare promontory, two hundred feet from
the regular rim wall, I felt isolated, marooned.

The sun, a liquid red globe, had just touched its under
side to the pink cliffs of Utah, and fired a crimson flood of
light over the wonderful mountains, plateaus, escarpments,
mesas, domes and turrets of the gorge. The rim wall of
Powell's Plateau was a thin streak of fire; the timber above
like grass of gold; and the long slopes below shaded from
bright to dark. Point Sublime, bold and bare, ran out
toward the plateau, jealously reaching for the sun. Bass's
Tomb peeped over the Saddle. The Temple of Vishnu lay
bathed in vapory shading clouds, and the Shinumo Altar
shone with rays of glory.

The beginning of the wondrous transformation, the
dropping of the day's curtain, was for me a rare and perfect
moment. As the golden splendor of sunset sought out a
peak or mesa or escarpment, I gave it a name to suit my
fancy; and as flushing, fading, its glory changed, sometimes
I rechristened it. Jupiter's Chariot, brazen wheeled, stood
ready to roll into the clouds. Semiramis's Bed, all gold,
shone from a tower of Babylon. Castor and Pollux clasped
hands over a Stygian river. The Spur of Doom, a mountain
shaft as red as hell, and inaccessible, insurmountable, lured
with strange light. Dusk, a bold, black dome, was shrouded
by the shadow of a giant mesa. The Star of Bethlehem

glittered from the brow of Point Sublime. The Wraith, fleecy, feathered curtain of mist, floated down among the ruins of castles and palaces, like the ghost of a goddess. Vales of Twilight, dim, dark ravines, mystic homes of specters, led into the awful Valley of the Shadow, clothed in purple night.

Suddenly, as the first puff of the night wind fanned my cheek, a strange, sweet, low moaning and sighing came to my ears. I almost thought I was in a dream. But the cañon, now blood-red, was there in overwhelming reality, a profound, solemn, gloomy thing, but real. The wind blew stronger, and then I was listening to a sad, sweet song, which lulled as the wind lulled. I realized at once that the sound was caused by the wind blowing into the peculiar formations of the cliffs. It changed, softened, shaded, mellowed, but it was always sad. It rose from low, tremulous, sweetly quavering sighs, to a sound like the last woeful, despairing wail of a woman. It was the song of the sea sirens and the music of the waves; it had the soft sough of the night wind in the trees, and the haunting moan of lost spirits.

With reluctance I turned my back to the gorgeously changing spectacle of the cañon and crawled in to the rim wall. At the narrow neck of stone I peered over to look down into misty blue nothingness.

That night Jones told stories of frightened hunters, and assuaged my mortification by saying "buck-fever" was pardonable after the danger had passed, and especially so in my case, because of the great size and fame of Old Tom.

"The worst case of buck-fever I ever saw was on a buffalo hunt I had with a fellow named Williams," went on Jones. "I was one of the scouts leading a wagon train west on the old Santa Fé trail. This fellow said he was a big hunter, and wanted to kill a buffalo, so I took him out. I saw a herd making over the prairie for a hollow where a brook ran, and by hard work, got in ahead of them. I picked out a position just below the edge of the bank, and we lay quiet, waiting. From the direction of the buffalo, I calculated we'd be just about right to get a shot at no very long range. As it was, I suddenly heard thumps on the ground, and cautiously raising my head, saw a huge buffalo bull just over us, not fifteen feet up the bank. I whispered to Williams: 'For God's sake, don't shoot, don't move!' The bull's little fiery eyes snapped, and he reared. I thought we were goners, for when a bull comes down on anything with his forefeet, it's done for. But he slowly settled back, perhaps doubtful. Then, as another buffalo came to the edge of the bank, luckily a little way from us, the bull turned broadside, presenting a splendid target. Then I whispered to Williams: 'Now's your chance. Shoot!' I waited for the shot, but none came. Looking at Williams, I saw he was white and trembling. Big drops of sweat stood out on his brow; his teeth chattered, and his hands shook. He had forgotten he carried a rifle."

"That reminds me," said Frank. "They tell a story over at Kanab on a Dutchman named Schmitt. He was very fond of huntin', an' I guess had pretty good success after deer an' small game. One winter he was out in the Pink Cliffs with a Mormon named Shoonover, an' they run into a lammin' big grizzly track, fresh an' wet. They trailed him to a clump of chaparral, an' on goin' clear round it, found no tracks leadin' out. Shoonover said Schmitt commenced to sweat. They went back to the place where the trail led in, an' there they were, great big silver-tip tracks, bigger'n hoss-tracks, so fresh thet water was oozin' out of 'em. Schmitt said: 'Zake, you go in und ged him. I hef took sick righdt now.'"

Happy as we were over the chase of Old Tom, and our prospects—for Sounder, Jude and Moze had seen a lion in a tree—we sought our blankets early. I lay watching the bright stars, and listening to the roar of the wind in the pines. At intervals it lulled to a whisper, and then swelled to a roar, and then died away. Far off in the forest a coyote barked once. Time and time again, as I was gradually sinking into slumber, the sudden roar of the wind startled me. I imagined it was the crash of rolling, weathered stone, and I saw again that huge outspread flying lion above me.

I awoke sometime later to find Moze had sought the warmth of my side, and he lay so near my arm that I reached out and covered him with an end of the blanket I used to break the wind. It was very cold and the time must have been very late, for the wind had died down, and I heard not a tinkle from the hobbled horses. The absence of the cowbell music gave me a sense of loneliness, for without it the silence of the great forest was a thing to be felt.

This oppressiveness, however, was broken by a far-distant cry, unlike any sound I had ever heard. Not sure of myself, I freed my ears from the blanketed hood and listened. It came again, a wild cry, that made me think first of a lost child, and then of the mourning wolf of the north. It must have been a long distance off in the forest. An interval of some moments passed, then it pealed out again, nearer this time, and so human that it startled me. Moze raised his head and growled low in his throat and sniffed the keen air.

"Jones, Jones," I called, reaching over to touch the old hunter.

He awoke at once, with the clear-headedness of the light sleeper.

"I heard the cry of some beast," I said, "and it was so weird, so strange. I want to know what it was."

Such a long silence ensued that I began to despair of hearing the cry again, when, with a suddenness which straightened the hair on my head, a wailing shriek, exactly like a despairing woman might give in death agony, split the night silence. It seemed right on us.

"Cougar! Cougar! Cougar!" exclaimed Jones.

"What's up?" queried Frank, awakened by the dogs.

Their howling roused the rest of the party, and no doubt scared the cougar, for his womanish scream was not repeated. Then Jones got up and gathered his blankets in a roll.

"Where you oozin' for now?" asked Frank sleepily.

"I think that cougar just came up over the rim on a scouting hunt, and I'm going to go down to the head of the trail and stay there till morning. If he returns that way, I'll put him up a tree."

With this, he unchained Sounder and Don, and stalked off under the trees, looking like an Indian. Once the deep bay of Sounder rang out; Jones's sharp command followed, and then the familiar silence encompassed the forest and was broken no more.

When I awoke all was gray, except toward the cañon, where the little bit of sky I saw through the pines glowed a delicate pink. I crawled out on the instant, got into my boots and coat, and kicked up the smoldering fire. Jim heard me, and said:

"Shore you're up early."

"I'm going to see the sunrise from the north rim of the Grand Cañon," I said, and knew when I spoke that very few men, out of all the millions of travelers, had ever seen this, probably the most surpassingly beautiful pageant in the world. At most, only a few geologists, scientists, perhaps an artist or two, and horse wranglers, hunters and prospectors have ever reached the rim on the north side; and these men, crossing from Bright Angel or Mystic Spring trails on the south rim, seldom or never get beyond Powell's Plateau.

The frost cracked under my boots like frail ice, and the bluebells peeped wanly from the white. When I reached the head of Clarke's trail it was just daylight; and there, under a pine, I found Jones rolled in his blankets, with Sounder and Moze asleep beside him. I turned without disturbing him, and went along the edge of the forest, but back a little distance from the rim wall.

I saw deer off in the woods, and tarrying, watched them throw up graceful heads, and look and listen. The soft pink glow through the pines deepened to rose, and suddenly I caught a point of red fire. Then I hurried to the place I had named Singing Cliffs, and keeping my eyes fast on the stone beneath me, crawled out to the very farthest point, drew a long, deep breath, and looked eastward.

The awfulness of sudden death and the glory of heaven stunned me! The thing that had been mystery at twilight, lay clear, pure, open in the rosy hue of dawn. Out of the gates of the morning poured a light which glorified the palaces and pyramids, purged and purified the afternoon's inscrutable clefts, swept away the shadows of the mesas, and bathed that broad, deep world of mighty mountains, stately spars of rock, sculptured cathedrals and alabaster terraces in an artist's dream of color. A pearl from heaven had burst, flinging its heart of fire into this chasm. A stream of opal flowed out of the sun, to touch each peak, mesa, dome, parapet, temple and tower, cliff and cleft into the new-born life of another day.

I sat there for a long time and knew that every second the scene changed, yet I could not tell how. I knew I sat high over a hole of broken, splintered, barren mountains; I knew I could see a hundred miles of the length of it, and eighteen miles of the width of it, and a mile of the depth of it, and the shafts and rays of rose light on a million glancing, many-hued surfaces at once; but that knowledge was no help to me. I repeated a lot of meaningless superlatives to myself, and I found words inadequate and superfluous. The spectacle was too elusive and too great. It was life and death, heaven and hell.

I tried to call up former favorite views of mountain and sea, so as to compare them with this; but the memory pictures refused to come, even with my eyes closed. Then I returned to camp, with unsettled, troubled mind, and was silent, wondering at the strange feeling burning within me.

Jones talked about our visitor of the night before, and said the trail near where he had slept showed only one cougar track, and that led down into the cañon. It had surely been made, he thought, by the beast we had heard. Jones signified his intention of chaining several of the hounds for the next few nights at the head of this trail; so if the cougar came up, they would scent him and let us know. From which it was evident that to chase a lion bound into the cañon and one bound out were two different things.

The day passed lamely, with all of us resting on the warm, fragrant pine-needle beds, or mending a rent in a coat, or working on some camp task impossible of commission on exciting days.

About four o'clock, I took my little rifle and walked off through the woods in the direction of the carcass where I had seen the gray wolf. Thinking it best to make a wide detour, so as to face the wind, I circled till I felt the breeze was favorable to my enterprise, and then cautiously approached the hollow where the dead horse lay. Indian

fashion, I slipped from tree to tree, a mode of forest travel
not without its fascination and effectiveness, till I reached
the height of a knoll beyond which I made sure was my
objective point. On peeping out from behind the last pine,
I found I had calculated pretty well, for there was the
hollow, the big windfall, with its round, starfish-shaped
roots exposed to the bright sun, and near that, the carcass.
Sure enough, pulling hard at it, was the gray-white wolf I
recognized as my "lofer."

But he presented an exceedingly difficult shot. Backing
down the ridge, I ran a little way to come up behind
another tree, from which I soon shifted to a fallen pine.
Over this I peeped, to get a splendid view of the wolf. He
had stopped tugging at the horse, and stood with his nose
in the air. Surely he could not have scented me, for the
wind was strong from him to me; neither could he have
heard my soft footfalls on the pine needles; nevertheless, he
was suspicious. Loth to spoil the picture he made, I risked
a chance, and waited. Besides, though I prided myself on
being able to take a fair aim, I had no great hope that I
could hit him at such a distance. Presently he returned to
his feeding, but not for long. Soon he raised his long,
fine-pointed head, and trotted away a few yards, stopped to
sniff again, then went back to his grewsome work.

At this juncture, I noiselessly projected my rifle barrel
over the log. I had not, however, gotten the sights in line
with him, when he trotted away reluctantly, and ascended
the knoll on his side of the hollow. I lost him, and had just
begun sourly to call myself a mollycoddle hunter, when he
reappeared. He halted in an open glade, on the very crest
of the knoll, and stood still as a statue wolf, a white,
inspiriting target, against a dark green background. I could
not stifle a rush of feeling, for I was a lover of the beautiful
first, and a hunter secondly; but I steadied down as the
front sight moved into the notch through which I saw the
black and white of his shoulder.

Spang! How the little Remington sang! I watched
closely, ready to send five more missiles after the gray
beast. He jumped spasmodically, in a half-curve, high in
the air, with loosely hanging head, then dropped in a heap.

I yelled like a boy, ran down the hill, up the other side of the hollow, to find him stretched out dead, a small hole in his shoulder where the bullet had entered, a great one where it had come out.

The job I made of skinning him lacked some hundred degrees the perfection of my shot, but I accomplished it, and returned to camp in triumph.

"Shore I knowed you'd plunk him," said Jim very much pleased. "I shot one the other day same way, when he was feedin' off a dead horse. Now thet's a fine skin. Shore you cut through once or twice. But he's only half lofer, the other half is plain coyote. Thet accounts fer his feedin' on dead meat."

My naturalist host and my scientific friend both remarked somewhat grumpily that I seemed to get the best of all the good things. I might have retaliated that I certainly had gotten the worst of all the bad jokes; but, being generously happy over my prize, merely remarked: "If you want fame or wealth or wolves, go out and hunt for them."

Five o'clock supper left a good margin of day, in which my thoughts reverted to the cañon. I watched the purple shadows stealing out of their caverns and rolling up about the base of the mesas. Jones came over to where I stood, and I persuaded him to walk with me along the rim wall. Twilight had stealthily advanced when we reached the Singing Cliffs, and we did not go out upon my promontory, but chose a more comfortable one nearer the wall.

The night breeze had not sprung up yet, so the music of the cliffs was hushed.

"You cannot accept the theory of erosion to account for this chasm?" I asked my companion, referring to a former conversation.

"I can for this part of it. But what stumps me is the mountain range three thousand feet high, crossing the desert and the cañon just above where we crossed the river. How did the river cut through that without the help of a split or earthquake?"

"I'll admit that is a poser to me as well as to you. But I suppose Wallace could explain it as erosion. He claims this whole western country was once under water, except the tips of the Sierra Nevada mountains. There came an uplift of the earth's crust, and the great inland sea began to run out, presumably by way of the Colorado. In so doing it cut out the upper cañon, this gorge eighteen miles wide. Then came a second uplift, giving the river a much greater impetus toward the sea, which cut out the second, or marble cañon. Now as to the mountain range crossing the cañon at right angles. It must have come with the second uplift. If so, did it dam the river back into another inland sea, and then wear down into that red perpendicular gorge we remember so well? Or was there a great break in the fold of granite, which let the river continue on its way? Or was there, at that particular point, a softer stone, like this limestone here, which erodes easily?"

"You must ask somebody wiser than I."

"Well, let's not perplex our minds with its origin. It is, and that's enough for any mind. Ah! listen! Now you will hear my Singing Cliffs."

From out of the darkening shadows murmurs rose on the softly rising wind. This strange music had a depressing influence; but it did not fill the heart with sorrow, only touched it lightly. And when, with the dying breeze, the song died away, it left the lonely crags lonelier for its death.

The last rosy gleam faded from the tip of Point Sublime; and as if that were a signal, in all the clefts and cañons below, purple, shadowy clouds marshaled their forces and began to sweep upon the battlements, to swing colossal wings into amphitheaters where gods might have warred, slowly to enclose the magical sentinels. Night intervened, and a moving, changing, silent chaos pulsated under the bright stars.

"How infinite all this is! How impossible to understand!" I exclaimed.

"To me it is very simple," replied my comrade. "The world is strange. But this cañon—why, we can see it all! I can't make out why people fuss so over it. I only feel peace. It's only bold and beautiful, serene and silent."

With the words of this quiet old plainsman, my sentimental passion shrank to the true appreciation of the scene. Self passed out to the recurring, soft strains of cliff song. I had been reveling in a species of indulgence, imagining I was a great lover of nature, building poetical illusions over storm-beaten peaks. The truth, told by one who had lived fifty years in the solitudes, among the rugged mountains, under the dark trees, and by the sides of the lonely streams, was the simple interpretation of a spirit in harmony with the bold, the beautiful, the serene, the silent.

He meant the Grand Cañon was only a mood of nature, a bold promise, a beautiful record. He meant that mountains had sifted away in its dust, yet the cañon was young. Man was nothing, so let him be humble. This cataclysm of the earth, this playground of a river was not inscrutable; it was only inevitable—as inevitable as nature herself. Millions of years in the bygone ages it had lain serene under a live moon; it would bask silent under a rayless sun, in the onward edge of time.

It taught simplicity, serenity, peace. The eye that saw only the strife, the war, the decay, the ruin, or only the glory and the tragedy, saw not all the truth. It spoke simply, though its words were grand: "My spirit is the Spirit of Time, of Eternity, of God. Man is little, vain, vaunting. Listen. To-morrow he shall be gone. Peace! Peace!"

14

All Heroes But One

As we rode up the slope of Buckskin, the sunrise glinted red-gold through the aisles of frosted pines, giving us a hunter's glad greeting.

With all due respect to, and appreciation of, the breaks of the Siwash, we unanimously decided that if cougars inhabited any other section of cañon country, we preferred it, and were going to find it. We had often speculated on the appearance of the rim wall directly across the neck of the cañon upon which we were located. It showed a long stretch of breaks, fissures, caves, yellow crags, crumbled ruins and clefts green with piñon pine. As a crow flies, it was only a mile or two straight across from camp, but to reach it, we had to ascend the mountain and head the cañon which deeply indented the slope.

A thousand feet or more above the level bench, the character of the forest changed; the pines grew thicker, and interspersed among them were silver spruces and balsams. Here in the clumps of small trees and underbrush, we began to jump deer, and in a few moments a greater number than I had ever seen in all my hunting experiences loped within range of my eye. I could not look out into the forest where an aisle or lane or glade stretched to any distance, without seeing a big gray deer cross it. Jones said the herds had recently come up from the breaks, where they had wintered. These deer were twice the size of the Eastern species, and as fat as well-fed cattle. They were almost as tame, too. A big herd ran out of one glade, leaving behind several curious does, which watched us intently for a moment, then bounded off with the stiff, springy bounce that so amused me.

Sounder crossed fresh trails one after another; Jude, Tige and Ranger followed him, but hesitated often, barked and whined; Don started off once, to come sneaking back at Jones's stern call. But surly old Moze either would not or could not obey, and away he dashed. Bang! Jones sent a charge of fine shot after him. He yelped, doubled up as if stung, and returned as quickly as he had gone.

"Hyar, you white and black coon dog," said Jones, "get in behind, and stay there."

We turned to the right after a while and got among shallow ravines. Gigantic pines grew on the ridges and in the hollows, and everywhere bluebells shone blue from the white frost. Why the frost did not kill these beautiful flowers was a mystery to me. The horses could not step without crushing them.

Before long, the ravines became so deep that we had to zigzag up and down their sides, and to force our horses through the aspen thickets in the hollows. Once from a ridge I saw a troop of deer, and stopped to watch them. Twenty-seven I counted outright, but there must have been three times that number. I saw the herd break across a glade, and watched them until they were lost in the forest. My companions having disappeared, I pushed on, and while working out of a wide, deep hollow, I noticed the sunny patches fade from the bright slopes, and the golden streaks vanish among the pines. The sky had become overcast, and the forest was darkening. "The Wranglers" I cried out returned in echo only. The wind blew hard in my face, and the pines began to bend and roar. An immense black cloud enveloped Buckskin.

Satan had carried me no farther than the next ridge, when the forest frowned dark as twilight, and on the wind whirled flakes of snow. Over the next hollow, a white pall roared through the trees toward me. Hardly had I time to get the direction of the trail, and its relation to the trees nearby, when the storm enfolded me. Of his own accord

Satan stopped in the lee of a bushy spruce. The roar in the pines equaled that of the cave under Niagara, and the bewildering, whirling mass of snow was as difficult to see through as the tumbling, seething waterfall.

I was confronted by the possibility of passing the night there, and calming my fears as best I could, hastily felt for my matches and knife. The prospect of being lost the next day in a white forest was also appalling, but I soon reassured myself that the storm was only a snow squall, and would not last long. Then I gave myself up to the pleasure and beauty of it. I could only faintly discern the dim trees; the limbs of the spruce, which partially protected me, sagged down to my head with their burden; I had but to reach out my hand for a snowball. Both the wind and snow seemed warm. The great flakes were like swan feathers on a summer breeze. There was something joyous in the whirl of snow and roar of wind. While I bent over to shake my holster, the storm passed as suddenly as it had come. When I looked up, there were the pines, like pillars of Pariar, marble, and a white shadow, a vanishing cloud fled, with receding roar, on the wings of the wind. Fast on this retreat burst the warm, bright sun.

I faced my course, and was delighted to see, through an opening where the ravine cut out of the forest, the red-tipped peaks of the cañon, and the vaulted dome I had named St. Marks. As I started, a new and unexpected after-feature of the storm began to manifest itself. The sun being warm, even hot, began to melt the snow, and under the trees a heavy rain fell, and in the glades and hollows a fine mist blew. Exquisite rainbows hung from white-tipped branches and curved over the hollows. Glistening patches of snow fell from the pines, and broke the showers.

In a quarter of an hour, I rode out of the forest to the rim wall on dry ground. Against the green piñons Frank's white horse stood out conspicuously, and near him browsed the mounts of Jim and Wallace. The boys were not in evidence. Concluding they had gone down over the rim, I dismounted and kicked off my chaps, and taking my rifle and camera, hurried to look the place over.

To my surprise and interest, I found a long section of

rim wall in ruins. It lay in a great curve between the two giant capes; and many short, sharp, projecting promontories, like the teeth of a saw, overhung the cañon. The slopes between these points of cliff were covered with a deep growth of piñon, and in these places descent would be easy. Everywhere in the corrugated wall were rents and rifts; cliffs stood detached like islands near a shore; yellow crags rose out of green clefts; jumble of rocks, and slides of rim wall, broken into blocks, massed under the promontories.

The singular raggedness and wildness of the scene took hold of me, and was not dispelled until the baying of Sounder and Don roused action in me. Apparently the hounds were widely separated. Then I heard Jim's yell. But it ceased when the wind lulled, and I heard it no more. Running back from the point, I began to go down. The way was steep, almost perpendicular; but because of the great stones and the absence of slides, was easy. I took long strides and jumps, and slid over rocks, and swung on piñon branches, and covered distance like a rolling stone. At the foot of the rim wall, or at a line where it would have reached had it extended regularly, the slope became less pronounced. I could stand up without holding on to a support. The largest piñons I had seen made a forest that almost stood on end. These trees grew up, down, and out, and twisted in curves, and many were two feet in thickness. During my descent, I halted at intervals to listen, and always heard one of the hounds, sometimes several. But as I descended for a long time, and did not get anywhere or approach the dogs, I began to grow impatient.

A large piñon, with a dead top, suggested a good outlook, so I climbed it, and saw I could sweep a large section of the slope. It was a strange thing to look down hill, over the tips of green trees. Below, perhaps four hundred yards, was a slide open for a long way; all the rest was green incline, with many dead branches sticking up like spars, and an occasional crag. From this perch I heard the hounds; then followed a yell I thought was Jim's, and after it the bellowing of Wallace's rifle. Then all was silent. The shots had effectually checked the yelping of the hounds. I let out a yell. Another cougar that Jones would not lasso! All at once I heard a familiar sliding of small rocks below me, and I watched the open slope with greedy eyes.

Not a bit surprised was I to see a cougar break out of the green, and go tearing down the slide. In less than six seconds, I had sent six steel-jacketed bullets after him. Puffs of dust rose closer and closer to him as each bullet went nearer the mark and the last showered him with gravel and turned him straight down the cañon slope.

I slid down the dead Piñon and jumped nearly twenty feet to the soft sand below, and after putting a loaded clip in my rifle, began kangaroo leaps down the slope. When I reached the point where the cougar had entered the slide, I called the hounds, but they did not come nor answer me. Notwithstanding my excitement, I appreciated the distance to the bottom of the slope before I reached it. In my haste, I ran upon the verge of a precipice twice as deep as the first rim wall, but one glance down sent me shudderingly backward.

With all the breath I had left I yelled: "Waa-hoo! Waa-hoo!" From the echoes flung at me, I imagined at first that my friends were right on my ears. But no real answer came. The cougar had probably passed along this second rim wall to a break, and had gone down. His trail could easily be taken by any of the hounds. Vexed and anxious, I signaled again and again. Once, long after the echo had gone to sleep in some hollow cañon, I caught a faint "Wa-a-ho-o-o!" But it might have come from the clouds. I did not hear a hound barking above me on the slope; but suddenly, to my amazement, Sounder's deep bay rose from the abyss below. I ran along the rim, called till I was hoarse, leaned over so far that the blood rushed to my head, and then sat down. I concluded this cañon hunting could bear some sustained attention and thought, as well as frenzied action.

Examination of my position showed how impossible it was to arrive at any clear idea of the depth or size, or condition of the cañon slopes from the main rim wall above. The second wall—a stupendous, yellow-faced cliff· two thousand feet high—curved to my left round to a point in front of me. The intervening cañon might have been a half mile wide, and it might have been ten miles. I had become disgusted with judging distance. The slope above this second wall facing me ran up far above my head; it fairly towered, and this routed all my former judgments, because I remembered distinctly that from the rim this yellow and green mountain had appeared an insignificant little ridge. But it was when I turned to gaze up behind me that I fully grasped the immensity of the place. This wall and slope were the first two steps down the long stairway of the Grand Cañon, and they towered over me, straight up a half-mile in dizzy height. To think of climbing it took my breath away.

Then again Sounder's bay floated distinctly to me, but it seemed to come from a different point. I turned my ear to the wind, and in the succeeding moments I was more and more baffled. One bay sounded from below, and next from far to the right; another from the left. I could not distinguish voice from echo. The acoustic properties of the amphitheater beneath me were too wonderful for my comprehension.

As the bay grew sharper, and correspondingly more significant, I became distracted, and focused a strained vision on the cañon deeps. I looked along the slope to the notch where the wall curved and followed the base line of the yellow cliff. Quite suddenly I saw a very small black object moving with snail-like slowness. Although it seemed impossible for Sounder to be so small, I knew it was he. Having something now to judge distance from, I conceived it to be a mile, without the drop. If I could hear Sounder, he could hear me, so I yelled with all my might. The echoes clapped back at me like so many slaps in the face. I watched the hound until he disappeared among broken heaps of stone, and long after that his bay floated to me.

Having rested, I essayed the discovery of some of my lost companions or the hounds, and began to climb. Before I started, however, I was wise enough to study the rim wall above, to familiarize myself with the break so I would have a landmark. Like horns and spurs of gold the pinnacles loomed up. Massed closely together, they were not unlike an astounding pipe-organ. I had a feeling of my littleness, that I was lost, and should devote every moment and effort to the saving of my life. It did not seem possible I could be hunting. Though I climbed diagonally, and rested often, my heart pumped so hard I could hear it. A yellow crag, with a round head like an old man's cane, appealed to me as near the place where I last heard from Jim, and toward it I labored. Every time I glanced up, the distance seemed the same. A climb which I decided would not take more than fifteen minutes, required an hour.

While resting at the foot of the crag, I heard more baying of hounds, but for my life I could not tell whether the sound came from up or down, and I commenced to feel that I did not much care. Having signaled till I was hoarse, and receiving none but mock answers, I decided that if my companions had not toppled over a cliff, they were wisely withholding their breath.

Another stiff pull up the slope brought me under the rim wall, and there I groaned, because the wall was smooth and shiny, without a break. I plodded slowly along the base, with my rifle ready. Cougar tracks were so numerous I got tired of looking at them, but I did not forget that I might meet a tawny fellow or two among those narrow passes of shattered rock, and under the thick, dark piñons. Going on in this way, I ran point-blank into a pile of bleached bones before a cave. I had stumbled on the lair of a lion and from the looks of it one like that of Old Tom. I flinched twice before I threw a stone into the dark-mouthed cave. What impressed me as soon as I found I was in no danger of being pawed and clawed round the gloomy spot, was the fact of the bones being there. How did they come on a slope where a man could hardly walk? Only one answer seemed feasible. The lion had made his kill one thousand feet above, had pulled his quarry to the rim and pushed it over. In view of the theory that he might have had to drag his victim from the forest, and that very seldom two lions worked together, the fact of the location of the bones was startling. Skulls of wild horses and deer, antlers and countless bones, all crushed into shapelessness, furnished indubitable proof that the carcasses had fallen from a great height. Most remarkable of all was the skeleton of a cougar lying across that of a horse. I believed—I could not help but believe that the cougar had fallen with his last victim.

Not many rods beyond the lion den, the rim wall split into towers, crags and pinnacles. I thought I had found my pipe organ, and began to climb toward a narrow opening in the rim. But I lost it. The extraordinarily cut-up condition of the wall made holding to one direction impossible. Soon I realized I was lost in a labyrinth. I tried to find my way down again, but the best I could do was to reach the verge of a cliff, from which I could see the cañon. Then I knew where I was, yet I did not know, so I plodded wearily back. Many a blind cleft did I ascend in the maze of crags. I could hardly crawl along, still I kept at it, for the place was conducive to dire thoughts. A tower of Babel menaced me with tons of loose shale. A tower that leaned more frightfully than the Tower of Pisa threatened to build my tomb. Many a lighthouse-shaped crag sent down little scattering rocks in ominous notice.

After toiling in and out of passageways under the shadows of these strangely formed cliffs, and coming again and again to the same point, a blind pocket, I grew desperate. I named the baffling place Deception Pass, and then ran down a slide. I knew if I could keep my feet I could beat the avalanche. More by good luck than management I outran the roaring stones and landed safely. Then rounding the cliff below, I found myself on a narrow ledge, with a wall to my left, and to the right the tips of piñon trees level with my feet.

Innocently and wearily I passed round a pillar-like corner of wall to come face to face with an old lioness and cubs. I heard the mother snarl, and at the same time her ears went back flat, and she crouched. The same fire of yellow eyes, the same grim snarling expression so familiar in my mind since Old Tom had leaped at me, faced me here.

My recent vow of extermination was entirely forgotten and one frantic spring carried me over the ledge.

Crash! I felt the brushing and scratching of branches, and saw a green blur. I went down straddling limbs and hit the ground with a thump. Fortunately, I landed mostly on

my feet, in sand, and suffered no serious bruise. But I was
stunned, and my right arm was numb for a moment. When
I gathered myself together, instead of being grateful the
ledge had not been on the face of Point Sublime—from
which I would most assuredly have leaped—I was the
angriest man ever let loose in the Grand Cañon.

Of course the cougars were far on their way by that
time, and were telling neighbors about the brave hunter's
leap for life; so I devoted myself to further efforts to find an
outlet. The niche I had jumped into opened below, as did
most of the breaks, and I worked out of it to the base of the
rim wall, and tramped a long, long mile before I reached
my own trail leading down. Resting every five steps, I
climbed and climbed. My rifle grew to weigh a ton; my feet
were lead; the camera strapped to my shoulder was the
world. Soon climbing meant trapeze work—long reach of
arm, and pull of weight, high step of foot, and spring of
body. Where I had slid down with ease, I had to strain and
raise myself by sheer muscle. I wore my left glove to tatters
and threw it away to put the right one on my left hand. I
thought many times I could not make another move; I
thought my lungs would burst, but I kept on. When at last
I surmounted the rim, I saw Jones, and flopped down
beside him, and lay panting, dripping, boiling, with
scorched feet, aching limbs and numb chest.

"I've been here two hours," he said, "and I knew things
were happening below; but to climb up that slide would kill
me. I am not young any more, and a steep climb like this
takes a young heart. As it was I had enough work. Look!"
He called my attention to his trousers. They had been cut
to shreds, and the right trouser leg was missing from the
knee down. His shin was bloody. "Moze took a lion along
the rim, and I went after him with all my horse could do. I
yelled for the boys, but they didn't come. Right here it is
easy to go down, but below, where Moze started this lion,
it was impossible to get over the rim. The lion lit straight
out of the piñons. I lost ground because of the thick brush
and numerous trees. Then Moze doesn't bark often enough.
He treed the lion twice. I could tell by the way he opened
up and bayed. The rascal coon-dog climbed the trees and

chased the lion out. That's what Moze did! I got to an open space and saw him, and was coming up fine when he went down over a hollow which ran into the cañon. My horse tripped and fell, turning clear over with me before he threw me into the brush. I tore my clothes, and got this bruise, but wasn't much hurt. My horse is pretty lame."

I began a recital of my experience, modestly omitting the incident where I bravely faced an old lioness. Upon consulting my watch, I found I had been almost four hours climbing out. At that moment, Frank poked a red face over the rim. He was in his shirt sleeves, sweating freely, and wore a frown I had never seen before. He puffed like a porpoise, and at first could hardly speak.

"Where—were—you—all?" he panted. "Say! but mebbe this hasn't been a chase! Jim an' Wallace an' me went tumblin' down after the dogs, each one lookin' out for his perticilar dog, an' darn me if I don't believe his lion, too. Don took one oozin' down the cañon, with me hot-footin' it after him. An' somewhere he treed that lion, right below me, in a box cañon, sort of an offshoot of the second rim, an' I couldn't locate him. I blamed near killed myself more'n once. Look at my knuckles! Barked 'em slidin' about a mile down a smooth wall. I thought once the lion had jumped Don, but soon I heard him barkin' again. All that time I heard Sounder, an' once I heard the pup. Jim yelled, an' somebody was shootin'. But I couldn't find nobody, or make nobody hear me. That cañon is a mighty deceivin' place. You'd never think so till you go down. I wouldn't climb up it again for all the lions in Buckskin. Hello, there comes Jim now."

Jim appeared just over the rim, and when he got up to us, dusty, torn and tagged out, with Don, Tige and Ranger showing signs of collapse, we all blurted out questions. But Jim took his time.

"Shore thet cañon is one hell of a place," he began finally. "Where was everybody? Tige and the pup went down with me an' treed a cougar. Yes, they did, an' I set under a piñon holdin' the pup, while Tige kept the cougar treed. I yelled an' yelled. After about an hour or two, Wallace came poundin' down like a giant. It was a sure thing we'd get the cougar; an' Wallace was takin' his picture when the blamed cat jumped. It was embarrassin', because he wasn't polite about how he jumped. We scattered some, an' when Wallace got his gun, the cougar was humpin' down the slope, an' he was goin' so fast an' the piñons was so thick thet Wallace couldn't get a fair shot, an' missed. Tige an' the pup was so scared by the shots they wouldn't take the trail again. I heard some one shoot about a million times, an' shore thought the cougar was done for. Wallace went pluggin' down the slope an' I followed. I couldn't keep up with him—he shore takes long steps—an' I lost him. I'm reckonin' he went over the second wall. Then I made tracks for the top. Boys, the way you can see an' hear things down in thet cañon, an' the way you can't hear an' see things is pretty funny."

"If Wallace went over the second rim wall, will he get back to-day?" we all asked.

"Shore, there's no tellin'."

We waited, lounged, and slept for three hours, and were beginning to worry about our comrade when he hove in sight eastward, along the rim. He walked like a man whose next step would be his last. When he reached us, he fell flat, and lay breathing heavily for a while.

"Somebody once mentioned Israel Putnam's ascent of a hill," he said slowly. "With all respect to history and a patriot, I wish to say Putnam never saw a hill!"

"Ooze for camp," called out Frank.

Five o'clock found us round a bright fire, all casting ravenous eyes at a smoking supper. The smell of the Persian meat would have made a wolf of a vegetarian. I devoured four chops, and could not have been counted in the running. Jim opened a can of maple sirup which he had been saving for a grand occasion, and Frank went him one better with two cans of peaches. How glorious to be hungry—to feel the craving for food, and to be grateful for it, to realize that the best of life lies in the daily needs of existence, and to battle for them!

Nothing could be stronger than the simple enumeration and statement of the facts of Wallace's experience after he left Jim. He chased the cougar, and kept it in sight, until it went over the second rim wall. Here he dropped over a precipice twenty feet high, to alight on a fan-shaped slide which spread toward the bottom. It began to slip and move by jerks, and then started off steadily, with an increasing roar. He rode an avalanche for one thousand feet. The jar loosened bowlders from the walls. When the slide stopped, Wallace extricated his feet and began to dodge the bowlders. He had only time to jump over the large ones or dart to one side out of their way. He dared not run. He had to watch them coming. One huge stone hurtled over his head and smashed a piñon tree below.

When these had ceased rolling, and he had passed down to the red shale, he heard Sounder baying near, and knew a cougar had been treed or cornered. Hurdling the stones and dead piñons, Wallace ran a mile down the slope, only to find he had been deceived in the direction. He sheered off to the left. Sounder's illusive bay came up from a deep cleft. Wallace plunged into a piñon, climbed to the ground, skidded down a solid slide, to come upon an impassable obstacle in the form of a solid wall of red granite. Sounder appeared and came to him, evidently having given up the chase.

Wallace consumed four hours in making the ascent. In the notch of the curve of the second rim wall, he climbed the slippery steps of a waterfall. At one point, if he had not been six feet five inches tall, he would have been compelled to attempt retracing his trail—an impossible task. But his height enabled him to reach a root, by which he pulled himself up. Sounder he lassoed *a la* Jones, and hauled up. At another spot, which Sounder climbed, he lassoed a piñon above, and walked up with his feet slipping from under him at every step. The knees of his corduroy trousers were holes, as were the elbows of his coat. The sole of his left boot—which he used most in climbing—was gone, and so was his hat.

15

Jones on Cougars

The mountain lion, or cougar, of our Rocky Mountain region, is nothing more nor less than the panther. He is a little different in shape, color and size, which vary according to his environment. The panther of the Rockies is usually light, taking the grayish hue of the rocks. He is stockier and heavier of build, and stronger of limb than the Eastern species, which difference comes from climbing mountains and springing down the cliffs after his prey.

In regions accessible to man, or where man is encountered even rarely, the cougar is exceedingly shy, seldom or never venturing from cover during the day. He spends the hours of daylight high on the most rugged cliffs, sleeping and basking in the sunshine, and watching with wonderfully keen sight the valleys below. His hearing equals his sight, and if danger threatens, he always hears it in time to skulk away unseen. At night he steals down the mountain side toward deer or elk he has located during the day. Keeping to the lowest ravines and thickets, he creeps upon his prey. His cunning and ferocity are keener and more savage in proportion to the length of time he has been without food. As he grows hungrier and thinner, his skill and fierce strategy correspondingly increase. A well-fed cougar will creep upon and secure only about one in seven of the deer, elk, antelope or mountain sheep that he stalks. But a starving cougar is another animal. He creeps like a snake, is as sure on the scent as a vulture, makes no more noise than a shadow, and he hides behind a stone or bush that would scarcely conceal a rabbit. Then he springs with terrific force, and intensity of purpose, and seldom fails to reach his victim, and once the claws of a starved lion touch flesh, they never let go.

A cougar seldom pursues his quarry after he has leaped and missed, either from disgust or failure, or knowledge that a second attempt would be futile. The animal making the easiest prey for the cougar is the elk. About every other elk attacked falls a victim. Deer are more fortunate, the ratio being one dead to five leaped at. The antelope, living on the lowlands or upland meadows, escapes nine times out of ten; and the mountain sheep, or bighorn, seldom falls to the onslaught of his enemy.

Once the lion gets a hold with the great forepaw, every movement of the struggling prey sinks the sharp, hooked claws deeper. Then as quickly as is possible, the lion fastens his teeth in the throat of his prey and grips till it is dead. In this way elk have carried lions for many rods. The lion seldom tears the skin of the neck, and never, as is generally supposed, sucks the blood of its victim; but he cuts into the side, just behind the foreshoulder, and eats the liver first. He rolls the skin back as neatly and tightly as a person could do it. When he has gorged himself, he drags the carcass into a ravine or dense thicket, and rakes leaves, sticks or dirt over it to hide it from other animals. Usually he returns to his cache on the second night, and after that the frequency of his visits depends on the supply of fresh prey. In remote regions, unfrequented by man, the lion will guard his cache from coyote and buzzards.

In sex there are about five female lions to one male. This is caused by the jealous and vicious disposition of the male. It is a fact that the old Toms kill every young lion they can catch. Both male and female of the litter suffer alike until after weaning time, and then only the males. In this matter wise animal logic is displayed by the Toms. The domestic cat, to some extent, possesses the same trait. If the litter is destroyed, the mating time is sure to come about regardless of the season. Thus this savage trait of the lions prevents overproduction, and breeds a hardy and intrepid race. If by chance or that cardinal feature of animal life—the survival of the fittest—a young male lion escapes to the weaning time, even after that he is persecuted. Young male lions have been killed and found to have had their flesh beaten until it was a mass of bruises and undoubtedly it had been the work of an old Tom. Moreover, old males and females have been killed, and found to be in the same bruised condition. A feature, and a conclusive one, is the fact that invariably the female is suckling her young at this period, and sustains the bruises in desperately defending her litter.

It is astonishing how cunning, wise and faithful an old lioness is. She seldom leaves her kittens. From the time they are six weeks old she takes them out to train them for the battles of life, and the struggle continues from birth to death. A lion hardly ever dies naturally. As soon as night descends, the lioness stealthily stalks forth, and because of her little ones, takes very short steps. The cubs follow, stepping in their mother's tracks. When she crouches for game, each little lion crouches also, and each one remains perfectly still until she springs, or signals them to come. If she secures the prey, they all gorge themselves. After the feast the mother takes her back trail, stepping in the tracks she made coming down the mountain. And the cubs are very careful to follow suit, and not to leave marks of their trail in the soft snow. No doubt this habit is practiced to keep their deadly enemies in ignorance of their existence. The old Toms and white hunters are their only foes. Indians never kill a lion. This trick of the lions has fooled many a hunter, concerning not only the direction, but particularly the number.

The only successful way to hunt lions is with trained dogs. A good hound can trail them for several hours after the tracks have been made, and on a cloudy or wet day can hold the scent much longer. In snow the hound can trail for three or four days after the track has been made.

When Jones was game warden of the Yellowstone National Park, he had unexampled opportunities to hunt cougars and learn their habits. All the cougars in that region of the Rockies made a rendezvous of the game preserve. Jones soon procured a pack of hounds, but as they had been trained to run deer, foxes and coyotes he had great trouble. They would break on the trail of these animals, and also on elk and antelope just when this was farthest from his wish. He soon realized that to train the hounds was a sore task. When they refused to come back at his call, he stung them with fine shot, and in this manner taught obedience. But obedience was not enough; the hounds must know how to follow and tree a lion. With this in mind, Jones decided to catch a lion alive and give his dogs practical lessons.

A few days after reaching this decision, he discovered the tracks of two lions in the neighborhood of Mt. Everett. The hounds were put on the trail and followed it into an abandoned coal shaft. Jones recognized this as his opportunity, and taking his lasso and extra rope, he crawled into the hole. Not fifteen feet from the opening sat one of the cougars, snarling and spitting. Jones promptly lassoed it, passed his end of the lasso round a side prop of the shaft, and out to the soldiers who had followed him. Instructing them not to pull till he called, he cautiously began to crawl by the cougar, with the intention of getting farther back and roping its hind leg, so as to prevent disaster when the soldiers pulled it out. He accomplished this, not without some uneasiness in regard to the second lion, and giving the word to his companions, soon had his captive hauled from the shaft and tied so tightly it could not move.

Jones took the cougar and his hounds to an open place in the park, where there were trees, and prepared for a chase. Loosing the lion, he held his hounds back a moment, then let them go. Within one hundred yards the cougar climbed a tree, and the dogs saw the performance. Taking a forked stick, Jones mounted up to the cougar, caught it under the jaw with the stick, and pushed it out. There was a fight, a scramble, and the cougar dashed off to run up another tree. In this manner, he soon trained his hounds to the pink of perfection.

Jones discovered, while in the park, that the cougar is king of all the beasts of North America. Even a grizzly dashed away in great haste when a cougar made his appearance. At the road camp, near Mt. Washburn, during the fall of 1904, the bears, grizzlies and others, were always hanging round the cook tent. There were cougars also, and almost every evening, about dusk, a big fellow would come parading past the tent. The bears would grunt furiously and scamper in every direction. It was easy to tell when a cougar was in the neighborhood, by the peculiar grunts and snorts of the bears, and the sharp, distinct, alarmed yelps of coyotes. A lion would just as lief kill a coyote as any other animal and he would devour it, too. As to the fighting of cougars and grizzlies, that was a mooted question, with the credit on the side of the former.

The story of the doings of cougars, as told in the snow, was intensely fascinating and tragical. How they stalked deer and elk, crept to within springing distance, then crouched flat to leap, was as easy to read as if it had been told in print. The leaps and bounds were beyond belief. The longest leap on a level measured eighteen and one-half feet. Jones trailed a half-grown cougar, which in turn was trailing a big elk. He found where the cougar had struck his game, had clung for many rods, to be dashed off by the low limb of a spruce tree. The imprint of the body of the cougar was a foot deep in the snow; blood and tufts of hair covered the place. But there was no sign of the cougar renewing the chase.

In rare cases cougars would refuse to run, or take to trees. One day Jones followed the hounds, eight in number, to come on a huge Tom holding the whole pack at bay. He walked to and fro, lashing his tail from side to side, and when Jones dashed up, he coolly climbed a tree. Jones shot the cougar, which, in falling, struck one of the hounds, crippling him. This hound would never approach a tree after this incident, believing probably that the cougar had sprung upon him.

Usually the hounds chased their quarry into a tree long before Jones rode up. It was always desirable to kill the animal with the first shot. If the cougar was wounded, and fell or jumped among the dogs, there was sure to be a terrible fight, and the best dogs always received serious injuries, if they were not killed outright. The lion would seize a hound, pull him close, and bite him in the brain.

Jones asserted that a cougar would usually run from a hunter, but that this feature was not to be relied upon. And a wounded cougar was as dangerous as a tiger. In his hunts Jones carried a shotgun, and shells loaded with ball for the cougar, and others loaded with fine shot for the hounds. One day, about ten miles from the camp, the hounds took a trail and ran rapidly, as there were only a few inches of snow. Jones found a large lion had taken refuge in a tree that had fallen against another, and aiming at the shoulder of the beast, he fired both barrels. The cougar made no sign he had been hit. Jones reloaded and fired at the head. The old fellow growled fiercely, turned in the tree and walked down head first, something he would not have been able to do had the tree been upright. The hounds were ready for him, but wisely attacked in the rear. Realizing he had been shooting fine shot at the animal, Jones began a hurried search for a shell loaded with ball. The lion made for him, compelling him to dodge behind trees. Even though the hounds kept nipping the cougar, the persistent fellow still pursued the hunter. At last Jones found the right shell, just as the cougar reached for him. Major, the leader of the hounds, darted bravely in, and grasped the leg of the beast just in the nick of time. This enabled Jones to take aim and fire at close range, which ended the fight. Upon examination, it was discovered the cougar had been half-blinded by the fine shot, which accounted for the ineffectual attempts he had made to catch Jones.

The mountain lion rarely attacks a human being for the purpose of eating. When hungry he will often follow the tracks of people, and under favorable circumstances may ambush them. In the park where game is plentiful, no one has ever known a cougar to follow the trail of a person; but outside the park lions have been known to follow hunters, and particularly stalk little children. The Davis family, living a few miles north of the park, have had children pursued to the very doors of their cabin. And other families relate similar experiences. Jones heard of only one fatality, but he believes that if the children were left alone in the woods, the cougars would creep closer and closer, and when assured there was no danger, would spring to kill.

Jones never heard the cry of a cougar in the National Park, which strange circumstance, considering the great number of the animals there, he believed to be on account of the abundance of game. But he had heard it when a boy in Illinois, and when a man all over the West, and the cry was always the same, weird and wild, like the scream of a terrified woman. He did not understand the significance of the cry, unless it meant hunger, or the wailing mourn of a lioness for her murdered cubs.

The destructiveness of this savage species was murderous. Jones came upon one old Tom's den, where there was a pile of nineteen elk, mostly yearlings. Only five or six had been eaten. Jones hunted this old fellow for months, and found that the lion killed on the average three animals a week. The hounds got him up at length, and chased him to the Yellowstone River, which he swam at a point impassable for man or horse. One of the dogs, a giant bloodhound named Jack, swam the swift channel, kept on after the lion, but never returned. All cougars have their peculiar traits and habits, the same as other creatures, and all old Toms have strongly marked characteristics, but this one was the most destructive cougar Jones ever knew.

During Jones's short sojourn as warden in the park, he captured numerous cougars alive, and killed seventy-two.

16

Kitty

It seemed my eyelids had scarcely touched when Jones's exasperating, yet stimulating, yell aroused me. Day was breaking. The moon and stars shone with wan luster. A white, snowy frost silvered the forest. Old Moze had curled close beside me, and now he gazed at me reproachfully and shivered. Lawson came hustling in with the horses. Jim busied himself around the campfire. My fingers nearly froze while I saddled my horse.

At five o'clock we were trotting up the slope of Buckskin, bound for the section of ruined rim wall where we had encountered the convention of cougars. Hoping to save time, we took a short cut, and were soon crossing deep ravines.

The sunrise coloring the purple curtain of cloud over the cañon was too much for me, and I lagged on a high ridge to watch it, thus falling behind my more practical companions. A far-off "Waa-hoo!" brought me to a realization of the day's stern duty, and I hurried Satan forward on the trail.

I came suddenly upon our leader, leading his horse through the scrub piñon on the edge of the cañon, and I knew at once something had happened, for he was closely scrutinizing the ground.

"I declare this beats me all hollow!" began Jones. "We might be hunting rabbits instead of the wildest animals on the continent. We jumped a bunch of lions in this clump of piñon. There must have been at least four. I thought first

175

we'd run upon an old lioness with cubs, but all the trails were made by full-grown lions. Moze took one north along the rim, same as the other day, but the lion got away quick. Frank saw one lion. Wallace is following Sounder down into the first hollow. Jim has gone over the rim wall after Don. There you are! Four lions playing tag in broad daylight on top of this wall! I'm inclined to believe Clarke didn't exaggerate. But confound the luck! the hounds have split again. They're doing their best, of course, and it's up to us to stay with them. I'm afraid we'll lose some of them. Hello! I hear a signal. That's from Wallace. Waa-hoo! Waa-hoo! There he is, coming out of the hollow."

The tall Californian reached us presently with Sounder beside him. He reported that the hound had chased a lion into an impassable break. We then joined Frank on a jutting crag of the cañon wall.

"Waa-hoo!" yelled Jones. There was no answer except the echo, and it rolled up out of the chasm with strange, hollow mockery.

"Don took a cougar down this slide," said Frank. "I saw the brute, an' Don was makin' him hump. A—ha! There! Listen to thet!"

From the green and yellow depths soared the faint yelp of a hound.

"That's Don! that's Don!" cried Jones. "He's hot on something. Where's Sounder? Hyar, Sounder! By George! there he goes down the slide. Hear him! He's opened up! Hi! Hi! Hi!"

The deep, full mellow bay of the hound came ringing on the clear air.

"Wallace, you go down. Frank and I will climb out on the pointed crag. Grey, you stay here. Then we'll have the slide between us. Listen and watch!"

From my promontory I watched Wallace go down with his gigantic strides, sending the rocks rolling and cracking; and then I saw Jones and Frank crawl out to the end of a crumbling ruin of yellow wall which threatened to go splintering and thundering down into the abyss.

I thought, as I listened to the penetrating voice of the hound, that nowhere on earth could there be a grander scene for wild action, wild life. My position afforded a commanding view over a hundred miles of the noblest and most sublime work of nature. The rim wall where I stood sheered down a thousand feet, to meet a long wooded slope which cut abruptly off into another giant precipice; a second long slope descended, and jumped off into what seemed the grave of the world. Most striking in that vast void where the long, irregular points of rim wall, protruding into the Grand Cañon. From Point Sublime to the Pink Cliffs of Utah there were twelve of these colossal capes, miles apart, some sharp, some round, some blunt, all rugged and bold. The great chasm in the middle was full of purple smoke. It seemed a mighty sepulcher from which misty fumes rolled upward. The turrets, mesas, domes, parapets and escarpments of yellow and red rock gave the appearance of an architectural work of giant hands. The wonderful river of silt, the blood-red, mystic and sullen Rio Colorado, lay hidden except in one place far away, where it glimmered wanly. Thousands of colors were blended before my rapt gaze. Yellow predominated, as the walls and crags lorded it over the lower cliffs and tables; red glared in the sunlight; green softened these two, and then purple and violet, gray, blue and the darker hues shaded away into dim and distinct obscurity.

Excited yells from my companions on the other crag recalled me to the living aspect of the scene. Jones was leaning far down in a niche, at seeming great hazard of life, yelling with all the power of his strong lungs. Frank stood still farther out on a cracked point that made me tremble, and his yell reënforced Jones's. From far below rolled up a chorus of thrilling bays and yelps, and Jim's call, faint, but distinct on that wonderfully thin air, with its unmistakable note of warning.

Then on the slide I saw a lion headed for the rim wall and climbing fast. I added my exultant cry to the medley, and I stretched my arms wide to that illimitable void and gloried in a moment full to the brim of the tingling joy of existence. I did not consider how painful it must have been to the toiling lion. It was only the spell of wild environment, of perilous yellow crags, of thin, dry air, of voice of man and dog, of the stinging expectation of sharp action, of life.

I watched the lion growing bigger and bigger. I saw Don and Sounder run from the piñon into the open slide, and heard their impetuous burst of wild yelps as they saw their game. Then Jones's clarion yell made me bound for my horse. I reached him, was about to mount, when Moze came trotting toward me. I caught the old gladiator. When he heard the chorus from below, he plunged like a mad bull. With both arms round him I held on. I vowed never to let him get down that slide. He howled and tore, but I held on. My big black horse with ears laid back stood like a rock.

I heard the pattering of little sliding rocks below; stealthy padded footsteps and hard panting breaths, almost like coughs; then the lion passed out of the slide not twenty feet away. He saw us, and sprang into the piñon scrub with the leap of a scared deer.

Samson himself could no longer have held Moze. Away he darted with his sharp, angry bark. I flung myself upon Satan and rode out to see Jones ahead and Frank flashing through the green on the white horse.

At the end of the piñon thicket Satan overhauled Jones's bay, and we entered the open forest together. We saw Frank glinting across the dark pines.

"Hi! Hi!" yelled the Colonel.

No need was there to whip or spur those magnificent horses. They were fresh: the course was open, and smooth as a racetrack, and the impelling chorus of the hounds was in full blast. I gave Satan a loose rein, and he stayed neck and neck with the bay. There was not a log, nor a stone, nor a gully. The hollows grew wider and shallower as we raced along, and presently disappeared altogether. The lion was running straight from the cañon, and the certainty that he must sooner or later take to a tree, brought from me a yell of irresistible wild joy.

"Hi! Hi! Hi!" answered Jones.

The whipping wind with its pine-scented fragrance, warm as the breath of summer, was intoxicating as wine. The huge pines, too kingly for close communion with their kind, made wide arches under which the horses stretched out long and low, with supple, springy, powerful strides. Frank's yell rang clear as a bell. We saw him curve to the right, and took his yell as a signal for us to cut across. Then we began to close in on him, and to hear more distinctly the baying of the hounds.

"Hi! Hi! Hi! Hi!" bawled Jones, and his great trumpet voice rolled down the forest glades.

"Hi! Hi! Hi! Hi!" I screeched, in wild recognition of the spirit of the moment.

Fast as they were flying, the bay and the black responded to our cries, and quickened, strained and lengthened under us till the trees sped by in blurs.

There, plainly in sight ahead ran the hounds, Don leading, Sounder next, and Moze not fifty yards behind a desperately running lion.

There are all-satisfying moments of life. That chase through the open forest, under the stately pines, with the wild, tawny quarry in plain sight and the glad staccato yelps of the hound filling my ears and swelling my heart, with the splendid action of my horse carrying me on the wings of the wind, was glorious answer and fullness to the call and hunger of a hunter's blood.

But as such moments must be, they were brief. The lion leaped gracefully into the air, splintering the bark from a pine fifteen feet up, and crouched on a limb. The hounds tore madly round the tree.

"Full-grown female," said Jones calmly, as we dismounted, "and she's ours. We'll call her Kitty."

Kitty was a beautiful creature, long, slender, glossy, with white belly and black-tipped ears and tail. She did not resemble the heavy, grimfaced brute that always hung in the air of my dreams. A low, brooding menacing murmur, that was not a snarl nor a growl, came from her. She watched the dogs with bright, steady eyes, and never so much as looked at us.

The dogs were worth attention, even from us, who certainly did not need to regard them from her personally hostile point of view. Don stood straight up, with his forepaws beating the air; he walked on his hind legs like the trained dog in the circus; he yelped continuously, as if it agonized him to see the lion safe out of his reach. Sounder had lost his identity. Joy had unhinged his mind and had made him a dog of double personality. He had always been unsociable with me, never responding to my attempts to caress him, but now he leaped into my arms and licked my face. He had always hated Jones till that moment, when he raised his paws to his master's breast. And perhaps more remarkable, time and time again he sprang up at Satan's nose, whether to bite him or kiss him, I could not tell. Then old Moze, he of Grand Cañon fame, made the delirious antics of his canine fellows look cheap. There was a small, dead pine that had fallen against a drooping branch of the tree Kitty had taken refuge in, and up this narrow ladder Moze began to climb. He was fifteen feet up, and Kitty had begun to shift uneasily, when Jones saw him.

"Hyar! you wild coon-chaser! Git out of that! Come down! Come down!"

But Jones might have been in the bottom of the cañon for all Moze heard or cared. Jones removed his coat, carefully coiled his lasso, and began to go hand and knee up the leaning pine.

"Hyar! dod-blast you, git down!" yelled Jones, and he kicked Moze off. The persistent hound returned, and followed Jones to a height of twenty feet, where again he was thrust off.

"Hold him, one of you!" called Jones.

"Not me," said Frank, "I'm lookin' out for myself."

"Same here," I cried, with a camera in one hand and a rifle in the other. "Let Moze climb if he likes."

Climb he did, to be kicked off again. But he went back. It was a way he had. Jones at last recognized either his own waste of time or Moze's greatness, for he desisted, allowing the hound to keep close after him.

The cougar, becoming uneasy, stood up, reached for another limb, climbed out upon it, and peering down, spat hissingly at Jones. But he kept steadily on with Moze close on his heels. I snapped my camera on them when Kitty was not more than fifteen feet above them. As Jones reached the snag which upheld the leaning tree, she ran out on her branch, and leaped into an adjoining pine. It was a good long jump, and the weight of the animal bent the limb alarmingly.

Jones backed down, and laboriously began to climb the other tree. As there were no branches low down, he had to hug the trunk with arms and legs as a boy climbs. His lasso hampered his progress. When the slow ascent was accomplished up to the first branch, Kitty leaped back into her first perch. Strange to say Jones did not grumble; none of his characteristic impatience manifested itself here. I supposed with him all the exasperating waits and vexatious obstacles were little things preliminary to the real work, to which he had now come. He was calm and deliberate, and slid down the pine, walked back to the leaning tree, and while resting a moment, shook his lasso at Kitty. This action fitted him, somehow; it was so compatible with his grim assurance.

To me, and to Frank, also, for that matter, it was all new and startling, and we were as excited as the dogs. We kept continually moving about, Frank mounted, and I afoot, to get good views of the cougar. When she crouched as if to leap, it was almost impossible to remain under the tree, and we kept moving.

Once more Jones crept up on hands and knees. Moze walked the slanting pine like a rope performer. Kitty began to grow restless. This time she showed both anger and impatience, but did not yet appear frightened. She growled low and deep, opened her mouth and hissed, and swung her tufted tail faster and faster.

"Look out, Jones! look out!" yelled Frank warningly.

Jones, who had reached the trunk of the tree, halted and slipped round it, placing it between him and Kitty. She had advanced on her limb, a few feet above Jones, and threateningly hung over. Jones backed down a little till she crossed to another branch, then he resumed his former position.

"Watch below," called he.

Hardly any doubt was there as to how we watched. Frank and I were all eyes, except very high and throbbing hearts. When Jones thrashed the lasso at Kitty we both yelled. She ran out on the branch and jumped. This time she fell short of her point, clutched a dead snag, which broke, letting her through a bushy branch from where she hung head downward. For a second she swung free, then reaching toward the tree caught it with front paws, ran down like a squirrel, and leaped off when thirty feet from the ground. The action was as rapid as it was astonishing.

Like a yellow rubber ball she bounded up, and fled with the yelping hounds at her heels. The chase was short. At the end of a hundred yards Moze caught up with her and nipped her. She whirled with savage suddenness, and lunged at Moze, but he cunningly eluded the vicious paws. Then she sought safety in another pine.

Frank, who was as quick as the hounds, almost rode them down in his eagerness. While Jones descended from his perch, I led the two horses down the forest.

This time the cougar was well out on a low spreading branch. Jones conceived the idea of raising the loop of his lasso on a long pole, but as no pole of sufficient length could be found, he tried from the back of his horse. The bay walked forward well enough; when, however, he got under the beast and heard her growl, he reared and almost threw Jones. Frank's horse could not be persuaded to go near the tree. Satan evinced no fear of the cougar, and without flinching carried Jones directly beneath the limb and stood with ears back and forelegs stiff.

"Look at that! look at that!" cried Jones, as the wary cougar pawed the loop aside. Three successive times did Jones have the lasso just ready to drop over her neck, when she flashed a yellow paw and knocked the noose awry. Then she leaped far out over the waiting dogs, struck the ground with a light, sharp thud, and began to run with the speed of a deer. Frank's cowboy training now stood us in good stead. He was off like a shot and turned the cougar from the direction of the cañon. Jones lost not a moment in pursuit, and I, left with Jones's badly frightened bay, got going in time to see the race, but not to assist. For several hundred yards Kitty made the hounds appear slow. Don, being swiftest, gained on her steadily toward the close of the dash, and presently was running under her upraised tail.

On the next jump he nipped her. She turned and sent him reeling. Sounder came flying up to bite her flank, and at the same moment fierce old Moze closed in on her. The next instant a struggling mass whirled on the ground. Jones and Frank, yelling like demons, almost rode over it. The cougar broke from her assailants, and dashing away leaped on the first tree. It was a half-dead pine with short snags low down and a big branch extending out over a ravine.

"I think we can hold her now," said Jones. The tree proved to be a most difficult one to climb. Jones made several ineffectual attempts before he reached the first limb, which broke, giving him a hard fall. This calmed me enough to make me take notice of Jones's condition. He was wet with sweat and covered with the black pitch from the pines; his shirt was slit down the arm, and there was blood on his temple and his hand. The next attempt began by placing a good-sized log against the tree, and proved to be the necessary help. Jones got hold of the second limb and pulled himself up.

As he kept on, Kitty crouched low as if to spring upon him. Again Frank and I sent warning calls to him, but he paid no attention to us or to the cougar, and continued to climb. This worried Kitty as much as it did us. She began to move on the snags, stepping from one to the other, every moment snarling at Jones, and then she crawled up. The big branch evidently took her eye. She tried several times to climb up to it, but small snags close together made her distrustful. She walked uneasily out upon two limbs, and as they bent with her weight she hurried back. Twice she did this, each time looking up, showing her desire to leap to the big branch. Her distress became plainly evident, a child could have seen that she feared she would fall. At length, in desperation, she spat at Jones, then ran out and leaped. She all but missed the branch, but succeeded in holding to it and swinging to safety. Then she turned to her tormentor, and gave utterance to most savage sounds. As she did not intimidate her pursuer, she retreated out on the branch, which sloped down at a deep angle, and crouched on a network of small limbs.

When Jones had worked up a little farther, he commanded a splendid position for his operations. Kitty was somewhat below him in a desirable place, yet the branch she was on joined the tree considerably above his head. Jones cast his lasso. It caught on a snag. Throw after throw he made with like result. He recoiled and recast nineteen times, to my count, when Frank made a suggestion.

"Rope those dead snags an' break them off."

This practical idea Jones soon carried out, which left him a clear path. The next fling of the lariat caused the cougar angrily to shake her head. Again Jones sent the noose flying. She pulled it off her back and bit it savagely.

Though very much excited, I tried hard to keep sharp, keen faculties alert so as not to miss a single detail of the thrilling scene. But I must have failed, for all of a sudden I saw how Jones was standing in the tree, something I had not before appreciated. He had one hand hold, which he could not use while recoiling the lasso, and his feet rested upon a precariously frail-appearing, dead snag. He made eleven casts of the lasso, all of which bothered Kitty, but did not catch her. The twelfth caught her front paw. Jones jerked so quickly and hard that he almost lost his balance, and he pulled the noose off. Patiently he recoiled the lasso.

"That's what I want. If I can get her front paw she's ours. My idea is to pull her off the limb, let her hang there, and then lasso her hind legs."

Another cast, the unlucky thirteenth, settled the loop perfectly round her neck. She chewed on the rope with her front teeth and appeared to have difficulty in holding it.

"Easy! Easy! Ooze thet rope! Easy!" yelled the cowboy.

Cautiously Jones took up the slack and slowly tightened the nose, then a quick jerk, fastened it close round her neck.

We heralded this achievement with yells of triumph that made the forest ring.

Our triumph was short-lived. Jones had hardly moved when the cougar shot straight out into the air. The lasso caught on a branch, hauling her up short, and there she hung in mid air, writhing, struggling and giving utterance to sounds terribly human. For several seconds she swung, slowly descending, in which frenzied time I, with ruling passion uppermost, endeavored to snap a picture of her.

The unintelligible commands Jones was yelling to Frank and me ceased suddenly with a sharp crack of breaking wood. Then crash! Jones fell out of the tree. The lasso streaked up, ran over the limb, while the cougar dropped pell-mell into the bunch of waiting, howling dogs.

The next few moments it was impossible for me to distinguish what actually transpired. A great flutter of leaves whirled round a swiftly changing ball of brown and black and yellow, from which came a fiendish clamor.

Then I saw Jones plunge down the ravine and bounce here and there in mad efforts to catch the whipping lasso. He was roaring in a way that made all his former yells merely whispers. Starting to run, I tripped on a root, fell prone on my face into the ravine, and rolled over and over until I brought up with a bump against a rock.

What a tableau riveted my gaze! It staggered me so I did not think of my camera. I stood transfixed not fifteen feet from the cougar. She sat on her haunches with body well drawn back by the taut lasso to which Jones held tightly. Don was standing up with her, upheld by the hooked claws in his head. The cougar had her paws outstretched; her mouth open wide, showing long, cruel, white fangs; she was trying to pull the head of the dog to her. Don held back with all his power, and so did Jones. Moze and Sounder were tussling round her body. Suddenly both ears of the dog pulled out, slit into ribbons. Don had never uttered a sound, and once free, he made at her again with open jaws. One blow sent him reeling and stunned. Then began again that wrestling whirl.

"Beat off the dogs! Beat off the dogs!" roared Jones. "She'll kill them! She'll kill them!"

Frank and I seized clubs and ran in upon the confused furry mass, forgetful of peril to ourselves. In the wild contagion of such a savage moment the minds of men revert wholly to primitive instincts. We swung our clubs and yelled; we fought all over the bottom of the ravine, crashing through the bushes, over logs and stones. I actually felt the soft fur of the cougar at one fleeting instant. The dogs had the strength born of insane fighting spirit. At last we pulled them to where Don lay, half-stunned, and with an arm tight round each, I held them while Frank turned to help Jones.

The disheveled Jones, bloody, grim as death, his heavy jaw locked, stood holding to the lasso. The cougar, her sides shaking with short, quick pants, crouched low on the ground with eyes of purple fire.

"For God's sake, get a half-hitch on the saplin'!"called the cowboy.

His quick grasp of the situation averted a tragedy. Jones was nearly exhausted, even as he was beyond thinking for himself or giving up. The cougar sprang, a yellow, frightful flash. Even as she was in the air, Jones took a quick step to one side and dodged as he threw his lasso round the sapling. She missed him, but one alarmingly outstretched paw grazed his shoulder. A twist of Jones's big hand fastened the lasso—and Kitty was a prisoner. While she fought, rolled, twisted, bounded, whirled, writhed with hissing, snarling fury, Jones sat mopping the sweat and blood from his face.

Kitty's efforts were futile; she began to weaken from the choking. Jones took another rope, and tightening a noose around her back paws, which he lassoed as she rolled over, he stretched her out. She began to contract her supple body, gave a savage, convulsive spring, which pulled Jones flat on the ground, then the terrible wrestling started again. The lasso slipped over her back paws. She leaped the whole length of the other lasso. Jones caught it and fastened it more securely; but this precaution proved unnecessary, for she suddenly sank down either exhausted or choked, and gasped with her tongue hanging out. Frank slipped the second noose over her back paws, and Jones did likewise with a third lasso over her right front paw. These lassoes Jones tied to different saplings.

"Now you are a good Kitty," said Jones, kneeling by her. He took a pair of clippers from his hip pocket, and grasping a paw in his powerful fist he calmly clipped the points of the dangerous claws. This done, he called to me to get the collar and chain that were tied to his saddle. I procured them and hurried back. Then the old buffalo hunter loosened the lasso which was round her neck, and as soon as she could move her head, he teased her to bite a club. She broke two good sticks with her sharp teeth, but the third, being solid, did not break. While she was chewing it Jones forced her head back and placed his heavy knee on the club. In a twinkling he had strapped the collar round her neck. The chain he made fast to the sapling. After removing the club from her mouth he placed his knee on her neck, and while her head was in this helpless position he dexterously slipped a loop of thick copper wire over her nose, pushed it back and twisted it tight. Following this, all done with speed and precision, he took from his pocket a piece of steel rod, perhaps one-quarter of an inch thick, and five inches long. He pushed this between Kitty's jaws, just back of her great white fangs, and in front of the copper wire. She had been shorn of her sharp weapons; she was muzzled, bound, helpless, an object to pity.

Lastly Jones removed the three lassoes. Kitty slowly gathered her lissom body in a ball and lay panting, with the same brave wildfire in her eyes. Jones stroked her black-tipped ears and ran his hand down her glossy fur. All the time he had kept up a low monotone, talking to her in the strange language he used toward animals. Then he rose to his feet.

"We'll go back to camp now, and get a pack-saddle and horse," he said. "She'll be safe here. We'll rope her again, tie her up, throw her over a pack-saddle, and take her to camp."

To my utter bewilderment the hounds suddenly commenced fighting among themselves. Of all the vicious bloody dog-fights I ever saw that was the worst. I began to belabor them with a club, and Frank sprang to my assistance. Beating had no apparent effect. We broke a dozen sticks, and then Frank grappled with Moze and I with Sounder. Don kept on fighting either one till Jones secured him. Then we all took a rest, panting and weary.

"What's it mean?" I ejaculated, appealing to Jones.

"Jealous, that's all. Jealous over the lion."

We all remained seated, men and hounds, a sweaty, dirty, bloody, ragged group. I discovered I was sorry for

Kitty. I forgot all the carcasses of deer and horses, the brutality of this species of cat; and even forgot the grim, snarling yellow devil that had leaped at me. Kitty was beautiful and helpless. How brave she was, too! No sign of fear shone in her wonderful eyes, only hate, defiance, watchfulness.

On the ride back to camp Jones expressed himself thus: "How happy I am that I can keep this lion and the others we are going to capture, for my own! When I was in the Yellowstone Park I did not get to keep one of the many I captured. The military officials took them from me."

When we reached camp Lawson was absent, but fortunately Old Baldy browsed near at hand, and was easily caught. Frank said he would rather take Old Baldy for the cougar than any other horse we had. Leaving me in camp, he and Jones rode off to fetch Kitty.

About five o'clock they came trotting up through the forest with Jim, who had fallen in with them on the way. Old Baldy had remained true to his fame—nothing, not even a cougar bothered him. Kitty, evidently no worse for her experience, was chained to a pine tree about fifty feet from the campfire.

Wallace came riding wearily in, and when he saw the captive, he greeted us with an exultant yell. He got there just in time to see the first special features of Kitty's captivity. The hounds surrounded her, and could not be called off. We had to beat them. Whereupon the six jealous canines fell to fighting among themselves, and fought so savagely as to be deaf to our cries and insensible to blows. They had to be torn apart and chained.

About six o'clock Lawson loped in with the horses. Of course he did not know we had a cougar, and no one seemed interested enough to inform him. Perhaps only Frank and I thought of it; but I saw a merry snap in Frank's eyes, and kept silent. Kitty had hidden behind the pine tree. Lawson, astride Jim's pack horse, a crochety animal, reined in just abreast of the tree, and leisurely threw his leg over the saddle. Kitty leaped out to the extent of her chain, an fairly exploded in a frightful cat-spit.

Lawson had stated some time before that he was afraid

of cougars, which was a weakness he need not have divulged in view of what happened. The horse plunged, throwing him ten feet, and snorting in terror, stampeded with the rest of the bunch and disappeared among the pines.

"Why the hell didn't you tell a feller?" reproachfully growled the Arizonian. Frank and Jim held each other upright, and the rest of us gave way to as hearty if not as violent mirth.

We had a gay supper, during which Kitty sat by her pine and watched our every movement.

"We'll rest up for a day or two," said Jones. "Things have commenced to come our way. If I'm not mistaken we'll bring an old Tom alive into camp. But it would never do for us to get a big Tom in the fix we had Kitty to-day. You see, I wanted to lasso her front paw, pull her off the limb, tie my end of the lasso to the tree, and while she hung I'd go down and rope her hind paws. It all went wrong to-day, and was as tough a job as I ever handled."

Not until late next morning did Lawson corral all the horses. That day we lounged in camp mending broken bridles, saddles, stirrups, lassoes, boots, trousers, leggins, shirts and even broken skins.

During this time I found Kitty a most interesting study. She reminded me of an enormous yellow kitten. She did not appear wild or untamed until approached. Then she slowly sank down, laid back her ears, opened her mouth and hissed and spat, at the same time throwing both paws out viciously. Kitty may have rested, but did not sleep. At times she fought her chain, tugging and straining at it, and trying to bite it through. Everything in reach she clawed, particularly the bark of the tree. Once she tried to hang herself by leaping over a low limb. When any one walked by her she crouched low, evidently imagining herself unseen. If one of us walked toward her, or looked at her, she did not crouch. At other times, noticeably when no one was near, she would roll on her back and extend all four paws in the air. Her actions were beautiful, soft, noiseless, quick and subtle.

The day passed, as all days pass in camp, swiftly and

pleasantly, and twilight stole down upon us round the ruddy fire. The wind roared in the pines and lulled to repose; the lonesome, friendly coyote barked; the bells on the hobbled horses jingled sweetly; the great watch stars blinked out of the blue.

The red glow of the burning logs lighted up Jones's calm, cold face. Tranquil, unalterable and peaceful it seemed; yet beneath the peace I thought I saw a suggestion of wild restraint, of mystery, of unslaked life.

Strangely enough, his next words confirmed my last thought.

"For forty years I've had an ambition. It's to get possession of an island in the Pacific, somewhere between Vancouver and Alaska, and then go to Siberia and capture a lot of Russian sables. I'd put them on the island and cross them with our silver foxes. I'm going to try it next year if I can find the time."

The ruling passion and character determine our lives. Jones was sixty-three years old, yet the thing that had ruled and absorbed his mind was still as strong as the longing for freedom in Kitty's wild heart.

Hours after I had crawled into my sleeping-bag, in the silence of night I heard her working to get free. In darkness she was most active, restless, intense. I heard the clink of her chain, the crack of her teeth, the scrape of her claws. How tireless she was. I recalled the wistful light in her eyes that saw, no doubt, far beyond the campfire to the yellow crags, to the great downward slopes, to freedom. I slipped my elbow out of the bag and raised myself. Dark shadows were hovering under the pines. I saw Kitty's eyes gleam like sparks, and I seemed to see in them the hate, the fear, the terror she had of the clanking thing that bound her.

I shivered, perhaps from the cold night wind which moaned through the pines; I saw the stars glittering pale and far off, and under their wan light the still, set face of Jones, and blanketed forms of my other companions.

The last thing I remembered before dropping into dreamless slumber was hearing a bell tinkle in the forest, which I recognized as the one I had placed on Satan.

17

Conclusion

Kitty was not the only cougar brought into camp alive. The ensuing days were fruitful of cougars and adventure. There were more wild rides to the music of the baying hounds, and more heart-breaking cañon slopes to conquer, and more swinging, tufted tails and snarling savage faces in the piñons. Once again, I am sorry to relate, I had to glance down the sights of the little Remington, and I saw blood on the stones. Those eventful days sped by all too soon.

When the time for parting came it took no little discussion to decide on the quickest way of getting me to a railroad. I never fully appreciated the inaccessibility of the Siwash until the question arose of finding a way out. To return on our back trail would require two weeks, and to go out by the trail north to Utah meant half as much time over the same kind of desert. Lawson came to our help, however, with the information that an occasional prospector or horse hunter crossed the cañon from the Saddle, where a trail led down to the river.

"I've heard the trail is a bad one," said Lawson, "an' though I never seen it, I reckon it could be found. After we get to the Saddle we'll build two fires on one of the high points an' keep them burnin' well after dark. If Mr. Bass, who lives on the other side, sees the fires he'll come down his trail next mornin' an' meet us at the river. He keeps a boat there. This is takin' a chance, but I reckon it's worth while."

So it was decided that Lawson and Frank would try to get me out by way of the cañon; Wallace intended to go by the Utah route, and Jones was to return at once to his range and his buffalo.

That night round the campfire we talked over the many incidents of the hunt. Jones stated he had never in his life come so near getting his "everlasting" as when the big bay horse tripped on a cañon slope and rolled over him. Notwithstanding the respect with which we regarded his statement we held different opinions. Then, with the unfailing optimism of hunters, we planned another hunt for the next year.

"I'll tell you what," said Jones. "Up in Utah there's a wild region called Pink Cliffs. A few poor sheep-herders try to raise sheep in the valleys. They wouldn't be so poor if it was not for the grizzly and black bears that live on the sheep. We'll go up there, find a place where grass and water can be had, and camp. We'll notify the sheep-herders we are there for business. They'll be only too glad to hustle in with news of a bear, and we can get the hounds on the trail by sun-up. I'll have a dozen hounds then, maybe twenty, and all trained. We'll put every black bear we chase up a tree, and we'll rope and tie him. As to grizzlies—well, I'm not saying so much. They can't climb trees, and they are not afraid of a pack of hounds. If we rounded up a grizzly, got him cornered, and threw a rope on him— there'd be some fun, eh, Jim?"

"Shore there would," Jim replied.

On the strength of this I stored up food for future thought and thus reconciled myself to bidding farewell to the purple cañons and shaggy slopes of Buckskin Mountain.

At five o'clock next morning we were all stirring. Jones yelled at the hounds and untangled Kitty's chain. Jim was already busy with the biscuit dough. Frank shook the frost off the saddles. Wallace was packing. The merry jangle of bells came from the forest, and presently Lawson appeared driving in the horses. I caught my black and saddled him, then realizing we were soon to part I could not resist giving him a hug.

An hour later we all stood at the head of the trail leading down into the chasm. The east gleamed rosy red. Powell's Plateau loomed up in the distance, and under it showed the dark-fringed dip in the rim called the Saddle. Blue mist floated round the mesas and domes.

Lawson led the way down the trail. Frank started Old Baldy with the pack.

"Come," he called, "be oozin' along."

I spoke the last good-by and turned Satan into the narrow trail. When I looked back Jones stood on the rim with the fresh glow of dawn shining on his face. The trail was steep, and claimed my attention and care, but time and time again I gazed back. Jones waved his hand till a huge jutting cliff walled him from view. Then I cast my eyes on the rough descent and the wonderful void beneath me. In my mind lingered a pleasing consciousness of my last sight of the old plainsman. He fitted the scene; he belonged there among the silent pines and the yellow crags.

ELMER KELTON

THE MAN WHO RODE MIDNIGHT

☐ 27713 $3.50

Bantam is pleased to offer these exciting Western adventures by ELMER KELTON, one of the great Western storytellers with a special talent for capturing the fiercely independent spirit of the West:

☐	25658	**AFTER THE BUGLES**	$2.95
☐	27351	**HORSEHEAD CROSSING**	$2.95
☐	27119	**LLANO RIVER**	$2.95
☐	27218	**MANHUNTERS**	$2.95
☐	27620	**HANGING JUDGE**	$2.95
☐	27467	**WAGONTONGUE**	$2.95
☐	25629	**BOWIE'S MINE**	$2.95
☐	26999	**MASSACRE AT GOLIAD**	$2.95
☐	25651	**EYES OF THE HAWK**	$2.95
☐	26042	JOE PEPPER	$2.95

"An American original."
—The New York Times Book Review

ELMORE LEONARD

For rugged stories of the American frontier, there is no writer quite like Elmore Leonard. Pick up these exciting westerns at your local bookstore—or use the handy coupon below for ordering.